Dear

Welcome [illegible] you have a wonderful year. Ms. Patterson

POLISHING THE APPLE:

TEACHER DEVOTIONS THAT OFFER BIBLICAL INSIGHTS FOR RESOLVING CONFLICTS AND IMPROVING SCHOOL RELATIONSHIPS

VOLUME 1

ELDERINE WYRICK

THE PRIDE

2013
MASTER'S PRIDE PRESS
CEDAR HILL, TEXAS

Teacher Devotions

Polishing the Apple, Volume 1 by Elderine Wyrick

Master's Pride Press
130 Bristol Drive
Cedar Hill, TX 75104

Pride logo and cover designed by Rik Wyrick, 2012. 2013.

Wyrick, Elderine W.

Polishing the Apple: Teacher devotions that offer Biblical insights for resolving conflicts and improving school relationships, Volume 1. Cedar Hill, TX: Master's Pride Press, 2013.

1.Teachers—Prayer and devotions. 2. Teachers—Attitude.
3. Teaching—Religious aspects—Christianity. I. Title

Dedication

I dedicate this book to my husband, Dean Wyrick, who supported me in the long, tedious hours required to write and edit the book. Much of the wisdom I gained came through his godly example and his consistent biblical counsel. Dean, you have changed my life through your spiritual leadership and your unconditional love of me . You are truly a gift from God that keeps on giving.

Acknowledgements

I want to thank Janet Munoz, Sharon Grey, John and Jane Evans, and Diane and Jay West for their comments and suggestions during the original editing process in 1998. I also want to thank Lynn Watson and Master's Academy's staff, Raymond and Sharon Jones, George Holder and his late wife, Rogene, my sister, Rene' Stone, my two sons, Rik and Russell, and my precious daughter-in-laws, Tracey and Theresa Wyrick who encouraged me, believed in me, and pushed me to fulfill the vision God placed in my heart.

TABLE OF CONTENTS

INTRODUCTION

James 3:1 *Not many of you should presume to be teachers, my you know that we who teach will be judged more strictly. brothers, because*

With red face and glaring eyes, she abruptly closed her book, pushed back the chair, stood up and declared, "I'm quitting! Any job would be better than this! I don't deserve this kind of treatment! Why would anybody put themselves through this kind of abuse?" And, as the startled students sat frozen in their seats, the first year teacher stomped out of the room to her principal's office where she promptly resigned.

I was that teacher over thirty years ago. I thought I was ready for the classroom, but I soon discovered a major gap in my preparation. I had not learned how to handle conflict. But, because of a wise, experienced principal, I didn't quit. She sent me home to pray and think about my situation. I was back the very next day! Returning to the classroom was like enrolling in *"Interpersonal Relationships 101".* As I learned to lean on the Spirit of God for instruction, life became my classroom, the Bible became my textbook, and experience became my practicum.

For centuries, the world has required a higher standard of conduct for teachers—especially those who work with children. Teachers are expected to be role models both at home and at school. Their response to conflict and life issues are scrutinized carefully by students, parents, neighbors, local citizens, and sometimes, even the entire nation when major events occur. Teachers shape the world of tomorrow. Teachers can cause students to "love" learning for the rest of their lives, or they can create memories of pain, rejection, and failure. They can also **"block" the quest for learning by planting seeds of** hopelessness and disdain for educators and school.

Nevertheless, some of us are called by God to be teachers. It is important that we acknowledge the fact that teachers are judged by a different standard—even higher standards than those required by city, state, or government leaders. James 3:1 tells us that teachers will receive greater judgment. Much attention has been given to the need for quality, well trained teachers. The world is crying out for higher academic standards. However, solid academic knowledge is not enough to produce a successful teacher.

Children from various backgrounds and experiences will fill our classrooms. We must be prepared to address these social differences including, economic status, religious background, cultural differences, parent's level of education, and philosophical tenets. Even this is not enough preparation for the teacher. Teachers should love their student during the discipline process. Nurturing acceptance and protective boundaries of discipline are needed for a stable learning environment. Without these two aspects—acceptance and a safe environment—the student will have entered into a year-long battle—a war zone of survival. While learning can take place under the worst of circumstances, stress and confusion caused from any conflict adversely affects the learning experience. Today's teacher must be prepared to face the challenge of teaching students how to build self-discipline and respect for others.

Overview of Book:

The pages of this book present the life messages of biblical conflict resolution and nuggets of wisdom I gained from over thirty years of practical classroom experience. I hope the reader finds it helpful in building godly relationships in an educational environment that contributes to making a real difference in the lives of their students.

The Bible gives instructions for managing interpersonal conflicts and serves as the foundation for devotions in this book. The devotions were written for my staff and are instructional in nature. They address issues of conflict that commonly occur in a teacher's day. Teachers, administrators, staff or others who work with people can use these daily devotions for guidance in handling professional, academic and personal conflicts in a way that pleases God and builds Christian character in their lives. Communities will profit when these truths are applied in their schools, and nations will benefit as biblical truths are again seen and heard in society.

A Subject Cross-Reference Index is included in the back of the book to assist readers in locating devotions that address specific topics. Teachers can choose devotions that will enlighten, instruct and encourage them as they struggle through specific issues such as appeal, disappointments, parent controversies, employer conflicts, and classroom friction.

Although this book specifically addresses school **issues, people from all walks of life can apply these nuggets** of truth to any job or personal situation. I have found the classroom to be the perfect "model" for explaining "cause and effect" in relationships such as marriage, family, church, and work related conflicts. The school setting allows us to see the "under-developed, undisciplined" child in personal interactions. It encourages us to turn from our "selfish and childish" attitudes that create rifts and unforgiveness in our relationships. We can learn to accept personal responsibility by humbly submitting to the scriptures and the truths designed to give us the true experience of "life, liberty and the pursuit of happiness."

I pray that these devotions will prove profitable to you and help you to gain fresh perspectives to your everyday experiences both in and out of the classroom.

1 HELP OUR STAFF TO FLOW TOGETHER

Ephesians 4:16 *From him the whole body, joined and held together by every supporting ligament, grows and builds itself up in love, as each part does its work.*

God has ordered your steps and placed you with specific people who may influence your future both personally and professionally. Perhaps you are thinking, "I don't think God sent Mr/s Doe! That teacher will never fit into our school. In fact, he/she seems strange."

1 Corinthians 12:21-26 *The eye cannot say to the hand, "I don't need you!" And the head cannot say to the feet, "I don't need you!"* 22 *On the contrary, those parts of the body that seem to be weaker are indispensable,* 23 *and the parts that we think are less honorable we treat with special honor. And the parts that are unpresentable are treated with special modesty,* 24 *while our presentable parts need no special treatment. But God has put the body together, giving greater honor to the parts that lacked it,* 25 *so that there should be no division in the body, but that its parts should have equal concern for each other.* 26 *If one part suffers, every part suffers with it; if one part is honored, every part rejoices with it.*

God "fitly" joins teams together (Ephesians 4:16). His purpose may be to trim off your rough edges through encounters with Mr./Ms. Doe. God may want you to learn how to love the unlovely. Or, you may experience a deeper walk of submission, unconditional love, or self-control through the things you suffer (Hebrews 5:8). Let Christ have His perfect work in you. Proverbs 3:34 tells us that God resists the proud but gives grace to the humble. God orders your footsteps. You can trust God in His choice of coworkers. Each person has something of value to offer. Ask yourself, "What was God's purpose in sending this coworker to me? What can I gain from working with him/her? What can he/she gain from working with me?" God will bless you for your teachable spirit and you may discover several life-changing nuggets of truth as you seek His purposes in this year's challenges. Let this year be a time of discovering God's purpose in your job assignment.

Dear God, Thank you for each staff member. Let me be a light set on a hill--a beacon pointing the way to you for those needing to find you. I submit myself as your servant in the position you have chosen for me. Help me to be pliable and teachable as you direct me through the year. Give me grace to teach and wisdom to learn from experience and instruction.

CR: Unity

2 WRITE THESE GOALS IN MY HEART

Proverbs 1:2-4 . . . *for gaining wisdom and instruction; for understanding words of insight; for receiving instruction in prudent behavior, doing what is right and just and fair; for giving prudence to those who are simple, knowledge and discretion to the young.*

Solomon names six purposes for the book of Proverbs

1. To teach wisdom (God's perspective on issues)
2. To gain instruction (natural laws of cause and effect)
3. To discover words of understanding (insight into God's Word and how it relates to current issues)
4. To accept *Instruction* in
   Wisdom –understanding God's character
   Justice—dealing with others in a righteous manner
   Judgment—knowing right from wrong and recognizing Satan's traps
   Equity--*teaching* values that will bring truth and balance to life
5. To give prudence to the simple (Teaching a foundation of truth so they will no longer be tossed *to and fro by every wind of doctrine*, philosophy, religion, or fad. Ephesians 4:14 (KJV)
6. To give knowledge and discretion (decision making ability based on truth, and understanding God's purpose and will.)

These six goals are imperative to our students' future. I encourage you to write these goals in your plan book and to review them often. Teachers should give students a foundation of truth that encourages right behavior, obedience, responsibility, and balance in everyday living. These acquired attributes will help to produce a happier, more congenial, and more productive society.

These truths are universal. The principles of Solomon can be taught without using the Bible or referring to God. They are universal truths that are applicable in every society, in every nation, and in all life experiences. They can be applied to work or play, to secular jobs, to profit or non-profit organizations, to public or private schools, and to individual family settings.

Dear God, Show me your truths and help me to teach those truths to my students. I submit myself to learn more of Christ's character so that I may become an example to my students.

3 HELP ME TO AVOID "SLANDER"

Psalms 15:1-3 *LORD, who may dwell in your sanctuary? Who may live on your holy hill? He whose walk is blameless and who does what is righteous, who speaks the truth from his heart and has no slander on his tongue, who does his neighbor no wrong and casts no slur on his fellowman .*

It is important to grasp the meaning of the word "slander" to fully understand scriptural instructions applicable to this destructive behavior. For the purpose of these devotions slander means "to dishonor, disgrace, humiliate, shame, or ruin someone's reputation through words, and/or gestures including "put downs." For those who want an "official definition" www.dictionary.com defines it "defamation by oral utterance." And www.biblegateway.com cross references "slander" with "backbiting, gossip, railing, speaking evil, talebearer, whisperer, deceivers, and liars".

Unfortunately, much of the comedy and entertainment in today's society hinges on slander or slurs. Americans, even children, mimic these comedians by repeating their sarcastic, cutting remarks at the expense of hurting others. Our "cuteness" and twist of words are cutting deep into the significance of those at work, at school and at home leaving wounds and scars that linger for an entire lifetime.

In times past, cutting words were used only against those we disdained and wanted to dishonor. In modern society, we expect even our youngest and most sensitive children to be "tough enough" to take it. Comedians and class clowns take pride in their ability to "crack a joke" using someone as the object of that joke. The "life" of the party is usually the most slanderous of the crowd. He is the guy who can point out every flaw, twist every statement, and relate every gesture to some underlying meaning. The entire group accepts him as "adorable" and acceptable while we hide our secret pain when he turns the joke on us. We feel ashamed if we let it hurt our feelings. We don't want to appear immature or weak.

At the risk of sounding stiff and "out of the flow", I propose that this "jesting" is nothing more than rudeness! Why has our society decided that this rudeness is acceptable and cute? Psalms 15 makes it clear that those who seek to dwell in God's sanctuary (His Secret Place) will not slander his brother. He will be sensitive to his brother's emotional needs and would never risk hurting him by using him as part of a joke. I wonder if we, without realizing it, have taken a detour to follow the path of those on the broad road. Slander does destroy. Think about it. Emotional wounds heal slowly. The pain can last a lifetime. Too many people are laughing on the outside and crying on the inside.

Dear God, Forgive me for accepting the world's perspective on put-downs and slams. Help me to realize the power of words as I teach and work with the students, staff, and parents of my school. Let my words be full of grace and life.

4 STUDENTS WANT ORDER

Proverbs 28:2 *When a country is rebellious, it has many rulers, but a ruler with discernment and knowledge maintains order.*

My first nine weeks as a classroom teacher seemed successful, but I wanted to do better. I decided to ask my junior high students to evaluate me. I said, "Take out a piece of paper and list three things you would change about my classroom if you were the teacher. Don't worry about what you write; I won't get upset with you. Please be honest."

Well, they were honest, and I was surprised at what they had to say. I received a total of forty-eight responses and forty-five responses said, "Make us be quiet so we can learn." I did not realize that my classroom was noisy. In fact, I was so busy "teaching" that I ignored most of what was happening in the classroom. I discovered that students were passing notes and talking throughout my entire lesson. I knew I had to make some changes, and I did. After I re-established the rules, I discovered the sound of a quiet classroom. I even became skilled at hearing noise.

This experience taught me that students care about order. They are uncomfortable with chaos, and they know they are not learning well when they goof off. The unexpected irony of their response was that the students who tested the boundaries were the students who put this suggestion as number one on their list. They wanted control. They needed discipline. They felt insecure with too much freedom.

Students learn best in an orderly, structured setting. Order and structure does not necessarily mean total silence, but it does mean that the teacher is always in control. Ignoring rowdiness can cause misbehavior. The ADHD child, who often over reacts, is especially vulnerable in an unstructured, chaotic classroom.

If needed, apologize to your class for not following the classroom rules. Review classroom policies and begin to enforce the rules. You will accomplish more teaching and have greater peace in your classroom.

Dear God, Help me to be consistent in my classroom discipline. Show me my weaknesses in this area and help me to produce the order and control that my students not only need but subconsciously want. Give me the courage to apologize and start again.

CR: Discipline, Leadership

5 MAKE MY CLASSROOM A SECURE PLACE

Psalms 91:4 *He will cover you with his feathers, and under his wings you will find refuge; his faithfulness will be your shield and rampart.*

English class began with the quick pop-up drill I commonly use before tests. Sitting near the front row, a young junior high girl jumped up to answer the question. When she got out of her seat, her half-slip fell around her feet. She instantly squatted to the floor concealing her slip with her skirt. Her eyes were wide with horror. She looked at me and silently cried, "Help!" with her eyes.

As I looked around, I realized that very few students saw what happened. "Class," I instructed. "Would everyone please close your eyes and put your head on your desk. Don't look around and don't ask any questions, please." Immediately the puzzled students did as I asked. After I saw all eyes closed, I nodded silently to the girl indicating with hand motions that she could step out of her slip and take it with her to the restroom. She left the room, and I invited the class to return to the drill. A few minutes later, she returned to the classroom restored and ready to participate in class. We never discussed this event.

Although this illustration initially seemed rather comical, I did not laugh during the ordeal. Instead, I felt a need to "cover" her with my guidance and direction. I knew she needed a refuge. For her, this was a major difficulty. It was not funny. It was embarrassing. The gratefulness in her eyes, and the hug she gave me later let me know I responded correctly.

This story touches my heart because it reminds me of times when I was embarrassed or felt ashamed. God was always there to offer me a place to run. He became my place of security. He gave me the courage to lick my wounds, to get up and to start again.

Work toward making your classroom a place of safety. Be prepared to offer a place of refuge for students who need to escape embarrassment or shame. Let the love of God flow through your actions as you determine to help the student caught in a trap.

Dear God, Thank you for the many times you brought me through embarrassment and shame. Make me sensitive to my students' needs and allow me to be faithful in shielding them when they need a place of refuge.

CR: Acceptance

6 SET ME FREE FROM ANGER

Matthew 18:21-22 *Then Peter came to Jesus and asked, "Lord, how many times shall I forgive my brother when he sins against me? Up to seven times?" [22]Jesus answered, "I tell you, not seven times, but seventy-seven times."*

Anger is a sign of unresolved issues. The root of anger can be masked, stuffed, or misplaced from earlier conflicts. Often we believe we have forgiven past hurts, when, in reality, we stuffed these hurts with the determined words of "I WILL forgive!" If you are unhappy or angry about life in general, you probably need to search your heart for unresolved issues.

Consider these questions to check for bitterness and anger. Do old wounds and offenses return when you least expect it? Do you stuff those feelings and tell yourself that you have already forgiven them? Do you feel uneasy when a certain person's name is mentioned? Do you avoid meeting or speaking to certain people? Do you carry secret guilt for being unable to release these wounds?

You are not God. Only God can instantly forgive. We must continue to work through our pain until the wounds heal. A cut is not healed until the pain is gone. Forgiveness is the same way. We must continue to forgive those who have wronged us until the pain goes away. Ignoring pain can create relationship problems with misplaced anger. Is the pain still there? Take your burden to the Lord, seventy times seven each day, and let Him teach you the meaning of true forgiveness. Jesus said, *Father, forgive them, for they do not know what they are doing* (Luke 23:34). It is essential that you continue to work toward forgiveness until you can honestly pray that prayer.

Forgiveness Exercise: Clasp your hands tight, visualize your offense/offender. Look toward heaven and pray, "Father, because you have forgiven me, I forgive ________. I release them in the name of Jesus. I let them go free." Open your hands symbolizing your release. Repeat this every time the offense comes to your mind. Choosing to let the offense go will set you free.

Dear God, Thank you for your ability to forgive me instantly, but I am unable to do the same for others. Help me to forgive ________. I know that only you can show me the way out of my anger into peace and forgiveness. Today and tomorrow and as long as it takes, I leave this pain at your feet choosing to forgive.

7 SHOW ME HOW TO TAKE EVERY THOUGHT CAPTIVE

2 Corinthians 10:5 *We demolish arguments and every pretension that sets itself up against the knowledge of God, and we take captive every thought to make it obedient to Christ.*

Our minds are amazing. We can re-create scenes from our past, or we can create new scenes that have never existed. We can remember and "hear" in our mind words of comfort, kindness, or hate that were said twenty years before. We can also imagine words said that we fear could be spoken. We can choose to think thoughts of goodness and become peaceful and happy or we can choose to think thoughts of hate and bitterness and become distraught and unhappy. We can change our thoughts instantly simply by switching channels like a television. We can control every thought; we can change our attitude by changing our minds.

Choose to put a guard over your thoughts and your mouth. Satan uses your mind as his battleground. His demonic forces buffet you with thoughts of insecurity, failure, unfairness, hopelessness, and accusations against the knowledge of God. Pull down every stronghold using scriptures and speaking the truth. Cast down every imagination and every negative thought. Do not allow yourself to dwell on what might happen; what should have happened; or why something did not happen.

Philippians 4:8 instructs us to think good thoughts. As we control our thoughts, we will also control the emotional climate around us. When we give only good reports, our joy and contentment will increase.

Dear God, Teach me to be a good warrior using your weapons of truth and love to pull down every stronghold that tries to destroy relationships within my school, my home, my church and my spiritual walk. Help me to recognize the battle within my own mind, and give me the courage to reject the thoughts that seek to destroy my day.

8 TEACH ME HOW TO HANDLE IRATE PARENTS

Proverbs 15:1 *A gentle answer turns away wrath, but a harsh word stirs up anger.*

If you expect a parent to call the school to complain, tell your principal. It is best that your principal know your side of the incident before the call comes. If you made a mistake, let your principal know. Your principal needs to be prepared to explain and support you during the initial contact. If a conference is scheduled, be determined to remain calm during the meeting. Anger belittles your position and takes away your control. Anytime a parent forcefully and loudly expresses their anger toward you, you will be tempted to answer them with the same tone and same force. However, as a professional, you should answer calmly, quietly, and professionally.

Unfortunately, parents can become angry and attack teachers when students slant reports in their favor. Often parents are responding to inaccurate information. If a parent becomes irate, first assume that there is a misunderstanding. This assumption will allow you deal with the conflict correctly. Truly listen to the parent's perspective. Let him/her finish the complaint without interruption or correction. Quietly check their message by saying something like, "I see that you are upset, and we do need to discuss this matter. However, I trust that we can handle this calmly since we both want what is best for your child. What I hear you saying is that you feel that I am picking on your child by giving a detention for something he/she didn't do. Is that correct?" Once the parent feels you have heard the complaint, he/she will be more willing to hear your answer. Your soft tone will also make it obvious how loud and harsh his/her own tone is.

If you are wrong, apologize. If the report is inaccurate, quietly explain the situation from your perspective. If the parent does not calm down, you should stand and say, "Mr./Mrs. Smith, perhaps we need to speak to the principal regarding this matter. Let's see if he/she is in the office." This is not a request, but it is a statement of your decision. Be assertive by walking toward the office and discontinuing the conversation. Do not continue a conference that has become unproductive or volatile.

The scriptures teach that a "soft answer" turns away wrath. Seek to be crucified with Christ and allow the Spirit of God to respond rather than your human nature.

Dear God, I need wisdom for times like these. Teach me to be like you, to think your thoughts, and to speak your words. Help me learn to speak softly in times of conflict.

CR: Communication

9 TEACH ME TO HONOR THE WISE AND CORRECT THE REBEL

Proverbs 19:25 *Flog* [discipline] *a mocker, and the simple will learn prudence; rebuke the discerning* [wise], *and they will gain knowledge.*
Proverbs 21:11 *When a mocker is punished, the simple gain wisdom; by paying attention to the wise they get knowledge.*

These proverbs identify three groups of people—the wise, the simple, and the mocker/scorner (rebel). Proverbs tells us that the wise student listens to instructions. He listens and learns from it. The wise are able and willing to learn from other people's insight without experiencing it themselves. The wise student has a heart to obey

Simple students are tossed about—not sure which way to turn; they can turn to the right or to the wrong way. They do not decide their direction until they see the teacher's response to misbehavior. If the teacher is consistent and true to the discipline policy, the simple will obey. If the teacher is inconsistent and allows the rebels (mockers) to rule the classroom, your simple students will join in the mockery. With consistent boundaries, the simple student will become wise (teachable) to avoid the consequences of misbehavior. The simple's response to authority depends upon the actions of the leader. They will either follow the wise or follow the mocker when they decide which side wins.

Mockers or Rebels must receive firm and quick correction. The only way you will gain wisdom in your classroom this year is to deal with the student who challenges your authority. Do not overlook little challenges—rolling eyes, smirks, put downs, innuendoes, partial obedience, and challenging questions regarding your knowledge or ability as a teacher. Ignoring the rebel or mocker is to allow him to duplicate himself throughout the year.

Make it a priority to give honor and praise to those who obey. As you acknowledge the positive things your students are doing, you will encourage correct behavior. When you reward the wise with appreciation and privileges, the simple students learn to obey. When you consistently deal with the rebel by giving him/her their earned consequences; the simple will usually reject the rebel. All students look for ways to feel significant and get attention. The mocker is seeking attention from his peers and his teacher when he acts out. He gets this attention through disobedience and negative behavior. If we correct the rebel but do not reward the wise for good behavior, the simple will follow the rebel who seems to be getting all of the attention. If we have positive rewards for correct behavior and negative consequences for incorrect behavior, the simple will choose the right direction.

Dear God, Give me the courage to be consistent and the wisdom to see mockery for what it is. Remind me to honor and acknowledge those students who are following directions and participating in class. Help me to lovingly apply discipline so that the simple can learn wisdom and the mocker can put away disobedience.

CR: Discipline, Scorner

10 TEACH ME TO NOT SIN WHEN I BECOME ANGRY

Ephesians 4:26-27 *In your anger do not sin": Do not let the sun go down while you are still angry,* [27]*and do not give the devil a foothold.*

Anger is a natural response to a perceived offense. It will come without invitation; you cannot stop it. Nevertheless, you can control your response to anger. The Bible does not say--do not become angry. It does say, "In your anger, do not sin." The "sin" is your inappropriate response--harboring an offense, refusing to forgive, cursing, rejecting, retaliating, slandering, pouting, or judging others' motives.

The first step in dealing with your anger is to admit that you are angry. You may need to get alone for a few minutes and consider the root of your anger. What right was violated? Was it the right to be obeyed, the right to be respected, the right to do what I want to do, the right to be told the truth, or the right to privacy? Identify your right. Next, nail your "right" to the cross of Christ; give it to Christ. We are crucified with Christ; therefore, our rights are also on the cross. Did you just say, "Wait, a minute! I have my rights!"?

When you gave your heart to Christ, you became a servant. Servants have responsibilities, not rights. Before you stop reading, please consider this truth further. Aren't we called to deny ourselves, take up our cross, and follow Christ? Please consider that we are not called to a self-centered, self-serving lifestyle, but rather to a lifestyle that serves our Heavenly Father and our fellow man. This can only be interpreted as 'responsibilities' rather than 'rights'.

Try to identify your responsibility to the student, parent, or coworker who has offended you. Is your responsibility simply to forgive? Is it to train, to correct, or to pray for those who mistreat you? Could it be to love your enemy? You may need to confront your offender with his error, or you may be the one who sinned and need to repent (Matthew 18; Matthew 5). As you consider the offense and the biblical perspective of your situation, choose to quiet your emotions and begin to deal rationally toward a solution that brings resolution and peace, not resentment and bitterness.

Remember, with God, all things are possible. God has a solution to your anger. Forgiveness and restoration are keys to peace and happiness. A responsible person takes action toward solutions not just toward peace.

Dear God, Teach me to lay down my rights and pick up my responsibilities. Help me to die to my flesh and choose responsibility over my rights. You are a servant; make me one too. I want to thank you for giving me clear thinking and a godly solution to this conflict.

CR: Rights, Forgiveness, Conflict

11 ALL TRUTH IS GOD'S TRUTH

John 8:31-32 . . . *Jesus said, "If you hold to my teaching, you are really my disciples. Then you will know the truth, and the truth will set you free."*

Throughout the four gospels Jesus said, "I tell you the truth..." or "Truly I say..." Over and over again Jesus emphasized that His word is truth--that His way was THE way--that His truth would set you free and give you a happier life.

Today, in modern society, many people believe that biblical teachings have no place in the "secular" world. Many believe our American society contains two sectors--a secular world and a religious world. Many insist that these two worlds are not compatible and should remain separate. However, this is completely contrary to the truth Christ taught. All truth is God's truth.

You may teach in a public school and still teach His truth. God's wisdom and His Word are principles of living--directions for doing right and turning from wrong. All of these truths can be shared openly without using the word "God" or without giving scripture and verse. Truths of kindness, concern for your fellowman, respect, responsibility, joyfulness, honesty, contentment, gentleness, and self-control can be openly trained in any classroom. Our secular world calls them "character traits." They are the principles of righteous living taught throughout the Bible.

Make character training one of the primary goals for your classroom. Your students will become better men and women because the truth will set them free from wrong behavior and bondage to self-centeredness.

Dear God, Teach me your ways that I might show others how to follow your truth. Let your truth dwell in me richly. I want your ways to become a natural outflow of my life.

12 DEVELOP THE ART OF FORGIVENESS AND RESTORATION IN ME

2 Samuel 9:8, 11 *Mephibosheth bowed down and said, 'What is your servant, that you should notice a dead dog like me? ...So Mephibosheth ate at David's table like one of the king's sons.*

The Bible considers dogs unclean animals. In fact, the vilest of sinners were often referred to as dogs. Mephibosheth was King Saul's grandson (Jonathan's son). When Saul's kingdom collapsed, a servant hid Mephibosheth to protect him from his grandfather's enemies. Several years later, Mephibosheth was discovered and brought to King David. Mephibosheth feared for his life because he was King Saul's grandson. He told David that he was a dead dog--"dead" because he was a useless cripple and unable to be a threat to David's kingdom--"dog" because he was bowing to the lowest position possible to plead for his life. What Mephibosheth did not know was that David wanted to exalt and honor Mephibosheth because of King David’s close friendship with his father, Jonathan. David exalted Mephibosheth and gave him a place in the palace and treated him like a king's son.

This famous Bible story reminds us of God's eternal work of salvation for each of us. We come before Him with all of our impurities deserving of death. He not only pardons us from our destruction, but He exalts us to the position of a king's son. Let the truth of what Jesus did at the cross sink deep into our hearts. Jesus died on the cross and offered “undeserved” forgiveness to us while we were YET in our sin.

As we allow this truth of "undeserved forgiveness" to become a reality in our lives, we will be equipped to forgive our students for their offenses even before they repent. "Blessed are the merciful, for they shall receive mercy" (Matt 5:7). David not only pardoned Mephibosheth; he also restored him to his position in the king's palace. When offenses occur in your classroom--correct, forgive, and then restore the student. Be Christ's hand extended. Be an example of God's love and grace.

Dear God, Let this truth be part of my daily life. I thank you for your forgiveness. Teach me to forgive and to restore.

13 ASK THEM! DON'T JUST TELL THEM!

Romans 14:13 *Therefore let us stop passing judgment on one another. Instead, make up your mind not to put any stumbling block or obstacle in your brother's way.*

I learned a valuable lesson during my first year of teaching from a quiet, well-mannered ninth grader. In fact, this is a story I tell students each year to illustrate the correct way to respond to a teacher when the teacher is wrong.

I was busy, as usual, rushing around the classroom trying to get my goals accomplished before the day was over. As I passed Dan's desk (not his real name), I said, "Dan, you have a detention for gum. You know you can't have gum in school." I hardly missed a step as I continued on to the front of the classroom to write down the detention.

Dan sat quietly and waited for an opportunity to speak with me. Later, I walked toward the back of the classroom near his desk. "Mrs. Wyrick, may I speak to you?" he asked in a soft tone. I nodded. He said, "Mrs. Wyrick, I wasn't chewing gum. Mr. Wilson gave me permission to have a cough drop."

I was embarrassed. I thanked him for his kindness and patience with me, and, of course, I quickly removed the detention from the record book. I was guilty of an assumption. I "told" him what he did wrong, rather than "asking" him if he had gum in his mouth. Although this gives a great example of how to appeal respectfully and quietly on the student's part, it is also an example of how "not" to approach a student who appears to be disobeying.

Not only will a question help clarify the child's intent. It also allows him to confess with his mouth when he is wrong. Confession is good for us all when we are wrong. When we are not wrong, it is good to have an opportunity to say so. Do not get too busy to deal with negative situations properly.

Dear God, Thank you for this valuable lesson. Remind me not to pass judgment on students when I don't have the details of the situation. CR: Discipline, Appeal

14 TEACH ME TO COVER OTHERS' FAULTS

1 Peter 4:8 *Above all, love each other deeply, because love covers over a multitude of sins.*

"Pointing out your failure makes me feel superior." This is a twisted thought that leads to slander and gossip. Can I truly love my fellowman and choose this destructive path? All humans are frail; we are all vulnerable; we have all sinned; we all have areas of weakness. Peter wrote that love covers these difficulties in others. Love takes no delight in revealing sin or "sharing" reports of failure or destruction. Love grieves and hurts when others fail. Love seeks to bind up the wounds, to support the weak, to protect the vulnerable, and to bring truth to the sinner. We must seek to love "deeply"-- deep enough to forgive faults, deep enough to restore our neighbor when he fails.

Covering a sin is not ignoring it. Rather, it is protecting our fellowman from destruction--from those who do not love him, from those who seek to destroy his reputation and his future, and from those who want to believe he is hopeless, helpless and cannot change. As we protect our brother from the "wolves," we must also lovingly confront the issues, appeal for change, and lead the student toward repentance. We must believe that change is possible and that, through Christ, the student can choose to turn from his error and be completely restored.

Matthew 18:15-17 gives us instructions for dealing with offenses. We, as teachers, should deal with our students privately when they fail. We must not argue, confront, or embarrass students in front of the class. When students believe you are their advocate, they will become more open to receive your counsel and your correction. Privacy is not always possible, but you can be careful not to shame the student as you discipline.

Love earns the right to discipline, the right to counsel, and the right to lead. This lesson also applies to relationships with fellow teachers. We must love our coworkers enough to support them in their weaknesses, and cover their faults before parents and students. Often parents, students, and teachers will bait us to see if we will participate in gossip toward church or school leaders, staff members, parents, students, or other teachers. Love does not discuss others' weaknesses; "love covers a multitude of sin." Love understands the Matthew 18 principle of going privately to someone in error for the purpose of restoration.

Dear God, Help me to be sensitive to the emotional needs of those I must correct. Give me the wisdom to deal with each person with honor, respect, and love.

CR: Discipline, Coworkers, Forgiveness, Slander, Love

15 LET WORDS OF LIFE COME OUT OF MY MOUTH TODAY

Proverbs 18:21 *The tongue has the power of life and death, and those who love it will eat its fruit.*

WORDS: Words can be irritating, exasperating, discouraging, devastating, and meddling; or they can be encouraging, life changing, discerning, supporting, and loving. Truly, *death and life are in the power of the tongue.*

"Sticks and stones may break my bones, but words can never hurt me." This old saying is not true. If I hit you with a stick, it may hurt you for a few minutes or even a few days, but in a short time the wound will heal and you will be free from every trace of the injury. However, if I call you names, belittle you, or shame you with my words, the wound can live in your memory and heart for the remainder of your life.

Scriptures tell us that we will give an answer for every careless word we speak (Matthew 12:36). We are reminded that it is better for us to be thrown into the deep sea than to cause a child to sin (Mark 9:42). We cannot afford to lose our temper or harbor resentment or bitterness toward one of our students.

Keep short accounts with your students. Clear offenses quickly. Pray for those who irritate you. Congenial students are easy to love but a teacher must purposefully determine to love the challenging students too. Allow the love of God to teach you how to love those students you find unlovely. God has promised that His grace is sufficient for you; he can take your lack of love and transform it into genuine love just by asking Him to do it. Do not live beneath God's promises. Let God's love permeate your heart for each student. Pray for unconditional love. God can and will miraculously answer your prayers. I know; I have personally experienced it. It works!

Why do we need genuine love for each student? Because I Corinthians 13:4-7 states *Love is patient, kind. ...It is not rude ...not self-seeking ...not easily angered ...It always protects, always trusts, always hopes, always perseveres.* These character traits will prepare teachers to lead their students into knowledge, self-acceptance, and determination to become all that they can be. Without love, the teacher is *nothing ...gain(s) nothing ...is like a resounding gong ...a clanging cymbal* (I Corinthians 13:1-3).

Dear God, Let blessing and not cursing come from my lips today. Remind me to ask for your supernatural love. Prick my heart with conviction if I mistreat my students. I want my heart to be a reflection of yours toward each child. Only you can accomplish such a colossal miracle in me. I submit myself to your miracle working power.

CR: Tongue, Love, Blessing, Anger, Heart Issues

16 DEAR GOD, I NEED TO CONFESS

Psalms 32:1, 5 *Blessed is the one whose transgressions are forgiven, whose sins are covered. ...I said, "I will confess my transgressions to the LORD"-- and you forgave the guilt of my sin.*

Lord, nothing is going right today. Everywhere I go someone seems offended. Did I speak too harshly? Was my look unkind? I did not mean to be. Somehow, I feel "off track"--a little off center. Help me, God! Forgive me! Cleanse me and set me back "on track." Give me grace and gentleness to deal with my students and coworkers. You and I both know where I missed your will. I am embarrassed. Teach me again, Father. *Create in me a clean heart, and renew a right spirit within me.* Psalms 51:10 (KJV). I thank you for your faithfulness.

As a teacher, I have learned that being "off track" is not a privilege that I can afford. One bad day can build walls with students and staff that may take weeks to tear down. Only the Spirit of God can give me the strength to change my attitude. He has promised His grace to me that can and will redirect my day.

If we want our students to follow a right path, we, as teachers, must constantly be aware of our personal response to God. Our attitudes and our sins affect our students. Remember Luke 6:40 *The student is not above the teacher, but everyone who is fully trained will be like their teacher.*

Dear God, never leave me in my sin. Constantly bring conviction and restoration to my life. I want to be your obedient servant. Change my heart, oh God.

CR: Heart Issues, Leadership, Attitude, LRA

17 LET ME SEE MY STUDENTS AS JESUS SEES THEM

1 Peter 5:2-3 *Be shepherds of God's flock that is under your care, serving as overseers--not because you must, but because you are willing, as God wants you to be; not greedy for money, but eager to serve [3] not lording it over those entrusted to you, but being examples to the flock.*

Have you learned to love your calling as a teacher? Have you chosen to praise God for the opportunity to be an overseer of his valuable possessions (the children)? When you see students through God's eyes, you will never be the same teacher you were before. Each child is precious to Him. Every student is a unique individual. Valuable potential is tucked inside; and God rejoices over each child with joy (Zephaniah 3:17).

Think of yourself as the jeweler assigned to shape precious diamonds--diamonds still in the rough, but destined to become the property of royalty. Each negative trait observed in the classroom is a positive trait not yet under the control of the Holy Spirit. A talker may be a future spokesperson, pastor, or teacher for the Kingdom of God. The student, who always wants to know why, may become an inventor, a teacher, or a prophet who proclaims truth to the nations. The meticulous, slower working child may become a financial manager, a designer or creator of new ideas or gadgets. The wiggly student may be the untiring evangelist that carries the Word of God across the nations, missionary, business owner, or chairman of the church property maintenance committee. The overly sensitive student may be a future caregiver or counselor in your community. The class clown may be an entertainer, a youth pastor, or an encourager in the body of Christ. As you work with your students this year, you may catch a dull sparkle of something great to come. Teachers must not stifle these natural traits, but rather train them (shape them) in the way that they should go (Proverbs 22:6). All of these traits can be positive strengths used for good and not bad. Help your students to discover these truths.

Through instruction and demonstration, you can lead your little flock closer to becoming the diamonds they were designed to be. Unconditional love, consistent training, and regular encouragement can polish rough edges quickly and you will begin to see glimpses of light sparkling through the "diamond in the making."

Dear God, Open my eyes and let me see your gifts in my students. Give me wisdom and direction for training each individual in the "path that they should go." Teach me to unselfishly and consistently train my students for your glory.
CR: Discipline, Love, Serve

18 HELP ME TO ACCEPT MY BOSS!

Romans 13:1 *Everyone must submit himself to the governing authorities, for there is no authority except that which God has established. The authorities that exist have been established by God.*

Understanding your position in the school is imperative to this year's success and daily contentment.

Each person in the school has an authority over them. Some may be thoughtful and kind while others may be harsh and unyielding. Whatever your situation, you can accept your leaders as God's gifts that He will use to train and develop you into the image of Christ. Often the most uncomfortable settings produce the greatest "nuggets of truth" needed for your future success.

It may be helpful to remember that those in authority over you deal with many other projects and problems not involving your grade or classroom. They are working with the "larger" picture of the school. You are only a section of that "larger picture." Therefore, misunderstanding or misjudging your authority's decisions is common. Do your students ever misunderstand or misjudge your decisions?

Teachers who learn to respect and follow their leaders will have a greater understanding of their role as an authority over their students. Understanding God's principles of authority is the foundation of building satisfying relationships at school. As a teacher "plants" seeds of obedience toward the principal, she will reap seeds of obedience from her students.

Dear God, Teach me to respect and obey my authority so that I may, in return, receive respect and obedience from my students.

CR: Respect, Leadership, Authority, Obedience

19 HELP ME TO BE HAPPY WHERE I AM PLANTED

Jeremiah 29:11 *"I know the plans I have for you," declares the Lord. " plans to prosper you, not to harm you, plans to give you hope and a future."*

God is in control of the times and places of this year. He gave you your assignment/job. He placed you on the staff, under the leaders and with the students that he chose for you. His purposes will become clear in time. His purpose could include one or more of the following reasons:

1. To give you a time of rest.
2. To give you opportunities
3. To learn new ideas and techniques in education.
4. To teach you the art of dying to your self-will and learn to serve and obey others with gladness.
5. To use conflict to knock off your rough edges. Proverbs 27:17 tells us, *As iron sharpens iron, so one person sharpens another.*
6. To teach you patience and tolerance as you learn to serve a personality who grates on your nerves.
7. To be an influence in someone's life as they observe your godly response to unfavorable circumstances;
8. To learn to love the unlovely, bless and not curse, to do good to those who are not necessarily good to you.
9. To grow in the art of forgiveness

You are a servant of Jesus Christ. He has assigned you to your job! Christ is in control of your present situation.

Rather than seeking a speedy release from the situation, determine to discover what lesson God has for you. Become all you can be in your present situation. Do not agitate your spirit with questions like--Why? or When? or How long? This will only bring emotional and physical fatigue and keep you in a state of disappointment. Learn to accept today's challenges with a determination to be the best you can be. Take control of your attitudes. Choose to look for the good and not the bad. You will have a better year and be a better person when the year ends.

The following is a part of the lyrics of the song, *I am Determined* written by Tim Sheppard. It encourages me to persevere.

When I am weary I'll look to His face;
And when I am tempted,
I'll trust in His grace...
I am determined to be invincible
'Til He has finished His purpose in me.
(Used by permission of Tim Sheppard)

Dear God, I choose to accept this year's assignment with gladness knowing that you have brought me to this place at this time for my good and not for evil. Help me to glean truth and knowledge from every situation I encounter, and teach me to say each day, "Not my will, but yours..."
CR: Obedience, Serve, Sacrifice

20 GIVE ME COURAGE TO CORRECT THE BULLY

Ephesians 4:31-32 *Get rid of all bitterness, rage and anger, brawling and slander, along with every form of malice. Be kind and compassionate to one another, forgiving each other, just as in Christ God forgave you.*

The tongue is sharp and destructive. Teachers and students often do not realize the damage their careless words can cause. I see students lose friendships because some "popular, tough guy" proclaims them (or their friend) to be "uncool," "weird," or "not with it." The bully expects the group to reject the "uncool" student. Unfortunately, students often pull away from the less popular kids because they fear being labeled "uncool" themselves. Where does that leave the "uncool" kid? They remain alone, isolated, insecure, rejected, and very vulnerable!

Be aware of students (or teachers) who use slander as a tool to control those around them. This behavior may stem from bitterness and pain in their personal lives. Unknowingly, they may want to inflict pain on others because of hurts they harbor in their own hearts. Bitterness is a disease that "seethes" out of a person and defiles those around them. (Hebrews 12:15). School leaders must confront these "personal attacks" that are so common in today's classrooms. To allow such behavior is to ignore the hurting cry of both the offender and the victim. The offender needs to understand how his verbal attacks affect his own life both socially and spiritually. No one really likes a bully unless he is a bully too. Although many students flock to the bully's side, they often do it from the fear of becoming his next victim, not from friendship. Being on the wrong side is the way of least resistance, and the majority of the students will follow unless they are trained to be sensitive to the needs of others. Being sensitive to others is good citizenship; being insensitive and unkind to others is rudeness.

Social issues are important in your school. A bully will duplicate himself! I urge you, as teachers who care for your students, to become involved with the issue of name calling and correct students who verbally bully others. It is important for students to respect their fellowman. They must understand that there will always be differences in people and these differences are good for us all. Training students to be responsible with their words offers an opportunity for them to see things from a different perspective. Help students to understand their involvement in bullying when they watch the bully and say or do nothing to protect the victim. Give students instructions on how to protect each other from being victimized. The bully gains power through the silence or cheers of his audience.

Predetermined consequences to name-calling should be an integral part of your discipline policy. Encourage your entire school to integrate the idea of "honoring" each other with kind words and appropriate actions! Name-calling, private jokes, or snide remarks should not be tolerated. (Psalms 15 gives God's perspective of bullying.) When the name calling and backbiting stops, your school becomes a “safer” place for students. They can discover the freedom of being themselves without having to be the toughest or coolest kid in school.

Dear God, Give me the courage to address the bully of the class. Help me to realize that I may be the instrument you placed in his life to help him overcome the inner rage and the wrong behavior that can eventually isolate him from friends and future success.

(Note: For further study, search Scriptures on mocker, slander, and strife. You may be surprised how much is written for dealing with those who attack others.) CR: bully, discipline, rage, backbiting, respect

21 WATCH OUT FOR THOSE WHO CAUSE DIVISION

Romans 16:17-18 *I urge you, brothers and sisters, to watch out for those who cause divisions and put obstacles in your way that are contrary to the teaching you have learned. Keep away from them. For such people are not serving our Lord Christ, but their own appetites.*

Satan's plan is to divide and conquer. It is simple. It works! Many good ministries collapse because people did not recognize Satan's tactics and his work among the Body of Christ. Divisions and obstacles come in many different brightly colored packages--discontent, gossip, slander, joking, false doctrine, unforgiveness, bitter words, rebellion, differing opinions, self-appointed "committees", idle talk, envy, jealously, pride, arrogance, desire for control, greed, imaginations, or "better or new ideas."

Anyone can fall into these traps. No one is exempt. We may be the perpetrator at one time and the victim at another. Beware! Be on guard! Satan roams about like a roaring lion seeking to devour us (1 Peter 5:8). It could be you, your friends, your coworkers, or your students!

Know those among you who create conflict and stir up bad attitudes. Avoid them if they are staff members. If they are students, correct them, and, if possible, remove them from the group if they refuse correction. It only takes one critical person to poison the attitude of a whole group. This poison spreads to one person at a time, but it will eventually drain the love, peace, and life out of the whole group if allowed to go unchecked. If you are not in a position to bring correction, then your instruction is to "*Keep away from them.*" Do not participate in their poisonous talk. Also, encourage others to turn away from the negative influences. It may even be necessary for you to let that person know that you do not want them calling you or speaking those things to you. Be bold! There are consequences for every decision. Listen to their poisonous words, and you will become like them; refuse to listen, and you will retain your inner joy and peace.

Dear God, Sometimes I am caught up in the negative. Forgive me and save me from the poisonous trap of division. I know unity is your goal for all of us. Teach me to stand boldly for right and to walk away from wrong. Amen.

CR: Discipline, Gossip, Conflict, Coworkers, Division

22 TEACH ME YOUR TRUTHS

John 8:32 ...*Then you will know the truth, and the truth will set you free.*

The world is full of controversy, extreme ideas (both to the left and to the right), contradicting religions and philosophies, and scattered values of right and wrong. Many (along with Caesar Augustus) are asking, "What is Truth?"

Professors and teachers promote the philosophy of Secular Humanism in classrooms throughout our nation. These teachers declare there is "no absolute truth" and promote it as an absolute truth. They teach that there is no absolute right or wrong. They believe "right and wrong" change with each situation. Their situational ethics discusses questions like "When is it right to lie?" or "Is stealing always wrong?" Secular Humanists discuss situations involving hardships and dangers and discuss how it might be okay to do what we normally think is "wrong." It sounds so logical. Christian teachers, parents, and students, even when they know the Word of God, have believed these "lies" about the truth.

How can a wrong make a right? This is a double-minded perspective--a forked tongue philosophy. Truth is truth, and a lie is a lie. Jesus said that the truth would set us free. Therefore, we must not believe that a lie is ever better than the truth. Satan is the deceiver, the manipulator, the twister of truth, and the half-truth teller. We must not embrace the "secular" philosophy of situational ethics. There is no truth separate from God's truth; therefore, there is no "secular" truth different from "religious" truth. All truth is God's truth.

Re-evaluate your own personal philosophies and make sure that you have only true philosophies--truths that agree with God's Word. False ideas can so easily attach to your way of thinking, especially as you sit under the "counsel" or teaching of the ungodly. Ask God to reveal these "errors" in your thinking. As He does, you will see more clearly how to lead others.

Remember that the truth sets people free to be all they can be--even when the truth hurts. It is best to say nothing rather than to speak falsely. God can give you wisdom in knowing how to answer each situation. God's guidance is just a whispered prayer away. Today, I urge you to commit to the truth. Be gentle as you speak the truth, but strive to be truthful.

Dear God, I want to know the truth and I want to speak the truth. Set a guard over my tongue that I may only speak truth. Cleanse my mind and heart of vain philosophies that do not agree with your Word. "Sanctify them (us) *through thy truth: thy word is truth."* John 17:17 *(KJV)*
CR: Truth, Thoughts, Tongue

23 CONFLICTS ARE OFTEN MISUNDERSTANDINGS

Job 34:32 *Teach me what I cannot see; if I have done wrong, I will not do so again.*

One day my husband discovered that our boys had opened two boxes of Corn Flakes. To save cabinet space, he began to combine the two boxes. My youngest son saw what he was doing and asked, "Dad, are you looking for the prize?" My husband chuckled and realized that he and my son could be doing the very same action and have two completely different reasons for doing it. You cannot always know the motives of the heart by a person's actions or words.

We all have blind spots. We can be unaware of our errors in a disagreement. We can be misunderstood. We can misunderstand others. Because of this, it is easy to misjudge one another, and have disagreements and conflicts.

If someone gives a bad report about you or makes a false accusation toward you, keep an open mind and allow room for miscommunications. Be prepared to listen to those involved in the conflict. Listen for things that you may have done wrong. If you see error—even a little bit, ask for forgiveness. Clear the beam out of your own eye first. Then, forgive them for their part. You only have control of your part of the conflict, but be determined to come to a peaceful solution as much as it depends upon you. This will bring honor to God.

After the conflict is settled, make a promise with those involved that you will refuse to think about the situation again. It is also best that you agree not to talk about the conflict to your offender or to others again. Promise to never bring it up again. Don't rekindle the fire.

Do not allow old re-runs of the conflict into your thoughts. Learn to change channels on your mental TV screen. You can control your thoughts. When your adversary confesses and repents, you need to make an effort to put the issue out of your mind. Sometimes, this is easier said than done. Nevertheless, with commitment and continuous forgiveness, most offenses will gradually fade. Forgiveness is a process. (You may need to see a counselor to work through extremely personal offenses. These offenses sometimes require professional help before you can truly be free of the pain.)

Dear God, Teach me to use your truth and your love to pull down every stronghold that tries to destroy relationships within my school, my home, and my church. Help me to recognize the battle within my own mind, and give me the courage to reject the thoughts that seek to destroy my day.
CR: Truth, Forgiveness, Thoughts, Communication, Parents, Conflict, Coworkers

24 MAY MY LOVE FOR YOU BE SEEN BY OTHERS

John 14:15 *If you love me, keep my commands.*

Most young children obey their parents because they fear the consequences of not obeying. They test limits to discover the consequences of each infraction. After their curiosity is satisfied, and they understand the borders, most will feel secure and resign themselves to remaining within those limits until a new issue arises. Their resignation directly links to the consistent consequence they find when they disobey. If the consequence is sometimes given and other times not given, the student will continue to test that issue. They have a need to know there is a boundary.

As children mature into young adults, a change takes place in their motivation for obeying. A respect and genuine love for parents often replaces the childhood fear. They begin to obey their parents out of respect and a desire to honor their mom and dad rather than out of the fear of punishment. This is what the Scripture means—"If you love me, you will obey what I command." A mature person, who has set aside the rebellion of their teenage years, will joyfully follow the directives of the one who has earned their love and respect. They know that blessing will be the result. Willful obedience based upon love instead of fear is due to developed trust!

Do you trust God enough to believe that He always leads the steps of the righteous? He has promised that he will never leave us nor forsake us (Deuteronomy 31:8). He has promised a long and abundant life to those who obey (Deuteronomy 6:2). God knows every detail of our lives and watches over us more than He takes care of the sparrows (Matthew 10:29-31).

If you trust God, it will be evident in your life. As you confidently walk through your day, be willing to accept the things that you cannot change. Your love for God will shine into your world. If you say you love the Lord, but you continually break the "rules," rebel against leadership, and purposely disregard biblical commands, you do not understand love. Jesus said that if we love Him, we will (a choice) obey (do) what He commanded. A person in love does not have to proclaim it to observers. It will be obvious. You honor those you love. Allow God's love to penetrate every part of your life. Submit to His commands, and His love will flow freely throughout your day.

Dear God, Teach me to trust you that I may grow in a greater love relationship with you. Lord, I want to trust you more!

CR: Discipline, Communication, Heart issues, Love, Obedience

25 I WANT TO LOVE YOU MORE!

Matthew 22:37 *Jesus replied: "Love the Lord your God with all your heart and with all your soul and with all your mind."*

Love is an exciting experience for all of us. A person does not "fall" in love or out of love simply with a decision. It seems to just happen. Learning to love the Lord with all of our heart often relates to the amount of time we spend getting to know Him. Isn't it true that the more we understand someone the easier it is to care for them?

Today, meditate on God's goodness and majesty. Rather than seeking to love God more, let your cry be, "God let me know you more!" Study some of His traits--mercy, goodness, long-suffering, gentleness, peace, love, forgiveness, provision, protection, concern, rest, joy, creativity, strength, justice, and boldness. Next, meditate on the things He does in your life and write down your thoughts and insights in a journal. Let the greatest commandment (Matthew 22:37-40) come alive within your spirit allowing God's love to fill you to overflowing. Loving

God more will prepare you for the second greatest commandment of loving your neighbor as yourself.

Is there anger, resentment, bitterness, or unforgiveness in your heart toward someone today? Perhaps you do not understand God's love for you. Or, have you failed to develop a prayer time with Him that brings His love and power into your heart. Only God's love allows you to accept others unconditionally and gives you the ability to forgive. As we understand the unfailing and unconditional love and grace God extends to us, we will better overlook our neighbor's shortcomings and failures. The key to forgiving others and loving them unconditionally is to see our own desperate need for God.

Dear God, I want to know you more. Teach me to study your traits until my mental picture of who you are reflects your greatness and goodness. Let this reflection flow out of my life as a light in the darkness. Let your love have its perfect work in my life. Help me to forgive others as I fully grasp your unconditional forgiveness for me.

CR: Discipline, Communication, Heart issues, Love, Obedience

26 I WANT TO LEARN LOVING CORRECTION

Proverbs 28:23 *He who rebukes a man will in the end gain more favor than he who has a flattering tongue.*

Students complain about two types of teachers—teachers that don't offer encouragement and praise, and teachers who praise students but don't control the classroom. Students want order and discipline. Without it, they are insecure and unable to concentrate.

Two important parts of discipline are compliments and correction. Your compliments must not be flattery (false). Proverbs 29:5 tells how flattery spreads a net or a trap for people. Teachers must be truthful in all things--even in compliments. Your words can be life and health to a student if you always speak truth in love, enveloping that truth (if unpleasant) with truthful statements of praise. Use the Oreo cookie method of confrontation. The two cookies are positive statements and the negative confrontation sits in the middle. A positive statement plus (+), a gentle rebuke (-), plus (+) a positive statement equals (=) loving correction. An example might be as follows:

"Joe, it's great that you know so much about history. Your classroom discussion is a real asset to the class. However, you continue to speak out without raising your hand, and other students are not able to participate in the discussion. I understand that you are excited about knowing information that you can share, but other students may begin to resent your controlling the classroom discussion. You are an intelligent young man with so much potential, and I know that you can understand what I am saying and can correct your behavior. What do you think?"

Discipline is not negative although consequences are often included in the process. It can be the tool God uses to bond teachers and students into a loving, healthy, working relationship. When students and teachers understand their role in education and establish reasonable boundaries, the school year will progress successfully. Loving correction brings security, self-respect, loyalty, trust, and obedience. Understanding the positive results of correction encourages us to learn the art of loving and purposeful discipline.

Dear God, Teach me balance in my discipline--balance of compliments and rebuke all given in love. Help me to discipline "for" my student's benefit, not just mine.
CR: Discipline,Leadership

27 GRACE OR PANIC

2 Corinthians 12:9-10 *But he said to me, 'My grace is sufficient for you, for my power is made perfect in weakness.' Therefore, I will boast all the more gladly about my weaknesses, so that Christ's power may rest on me. [10] That is why, for Christ's sake, I delight in weaknesses, in insults, in hardships, in persecutions, in difficulties. For when I am weak, then I am strong.*

Tough times come to all of us. After you have prayed, planned, and determined your course of action, circumstances change, obstacles appear, tragedy strikes, the unexpected happens, and your plans become obsolete. How do you gracefully adjust your direction in mid-stream when your situation changes, and your dreams are shattered? It happens, and when it does, we must be prepared.

The school year was going well (as far as I knew) with only a few bumps here and there. It looked like a successful year. Christmas break came and everything changed. Among my coworkers and church friends, there were two suicide attempts and a nervous breakdown. In addition, I lost three staff members mid-term. It seemed everything was crumbling around me. I could feel panic enveloping me. As I cried out to God for help, I instantly knew that He offered me a choice. "Will you choose panic or will you choose my grace? You can hide under my wing and be protected by the 'Shadow of the Almighty' or you can react out of panic."

I chose grace. This began a full semester of holding on to the horns of the altar waiting on God. I spent many hours waiting in prayer seeking God's strength and direction. As I prayed with our school staff each morning, I encouraged them to choose grace. We held on tight to God's hand each day. The boat rocked wildly for several months, but we made it with God's grace. There were times that it looked like the storm would sink the ship. We even considered closing the school permanently. Nevertheless, God sustained us. The school year ended. All the people in distress were renewed and God made things beautiful again.

God is truly our shelter in the time of storms. He proved to be the rock where I could hide. He is the "glory and the lifter of my head." He is my All in All. Gratitude and praise fill my heart even now as I recall His faithfulness. He will be faithful to you too when the storms come if you will chose grace rather than panic.

Dear God, Thank you for your grace. I thank you for preserving us through this unusual attack. It is true. Even the darkness is not dark to you. It shines as the day when you are with us (Psalms 139:12). I will always be grateful and changed because of this experience.

28 HELP ME TO DISCOVER EACH GIFT

Proverbs 18:16 *A gift opens the way for the giver and ushers him into the presence of the great.*

God gives gifts or talents to each person. These God given abilities are developed and discovered as we mature. Some gifts are never opened. An unopened gift that sits on a shelf is either a package of expectation or a waste of something valuable. Until someone opens the gift and uses it, it is merely a shell of what might be or could have been. An unused gift is unused potential and cannot accomplish what God sent it to do.

Why would someone leave a gift unopened, unused, or undiscovered? Perhaps the fear of failure or fear of men causes us to shy away from new experiences. Neglect or procrastination can also produce a stale or undeveloped talent. Laziness or self-protection can stifle potential. Or, even a lack of awareness of its existence could be the cause. No matter which applies to us, we can push past our fears and insecurities and open all our "packages" of potential. We should try new things and take classes in areas we have never studied before. We will continue to develop as individuals only when we remain teachable and flexible. Different experiences, good or bad, can be opportunities to learn and grow if we determine to discover more about ourselves.

Comparison is a common pitfall that stunts the growth of our talents. Gifts are unique to each individual; they are our personal monograms stamped by God in our original design. Each unique talent adds variety and richness to our world. Comparison is always a trap. If we compare our weaknesses to another's strengths, we feel diminished. If we compare our strengths to another's weakness, we become proud. Proverbs 16:18 says, *Pride goes before a fall.* And, if we compare our strengths to other's strengths, we become critical and judgmental.

As you develop your interests, your greatest talents will become evident. These talents will then bring you to a position of influence for the Kingdom of God. Do not hide your talents! Let your light shine for Jesus. Seek to remain a student and learn from those around you. Be all you can be.

Dear God, Are there undiscovered gifts and talents in me? If so, I commit myself to discover them. Lead me to them and give me the courage to try new things.
CR: Comparison, Heart Issues, Leadership

29 LET MY SERVICE BE GENUINE

Colossians 3:22 *Slaves, obey your earthly masters in everything; and do it, not only when their eye is on you and to win their favor, but with sincerity of heart and reverence for the Lord.*

Do you know a "man-pleaser"? (See Colossians 3:22 KJV.) If you do, you will have no doubt who they are. When the boss is around, they work diligently; they smile broadly giving "lip service" of praise and agreement. However, when the boss is not around their quality of work diminishes or perhaps even stops. They often gossip, talk about the boss, or argue about the company's rules. A man- pleaser usually does not carry his share of the work. Neither does he do anything "extra." He only works when the "boss" is in sight.

God's ways are higher than man's ways. The Bible did not say that we should obey an authority because he has earned it. God wants us to obey our leaders because we fear God. A diligent worker is an honor to God. He not only shows his understanding of God's ways, but he also shows a quiet trust in the Lord by placing his life into God's hands. A godly worker works even when no one notices or appreciates his work. The Christian teacher should do their work "as unto the Lord."

Do you catch yourself looking to see if the principal is coming? Do you say or think the words, "Here comes the principal," with a quick check on your current behavior? If so, you may be a man-pleaser who is giving eye service only to look good. When you realize that everything you do is before God, the highest authority, the principal coming into your work area is not such a significant event. If your priority is to please the highest authority, you will never fail to please your principal.

Dear God, Help me to be a "God pleaser" and not a "man pleaser." As I please you and obey your word, others will usually be pleased too. "If God is for us, who can be against us?" (Romans 8:31)

CR: Heart Issues, Anger, Coworkers, Boss, Obedience, Anger

30 TEACH ME COMPLETE JOY THROUGH FORGIVENESS

1 John 1:4-7 *We write this to make our joy complete.* [5]*This is the message we have heard from him and declare to you: God is light; in him there is no darkness at all.* [6] *If we claim to have fellowship with him yet walk in the darkness, we lie and do not live by the truth.* [7] *But if we walk in the light, as he is in the light, we have fellowship with one another, and the blood of Jesus, his Son, purifies us from all sin.*

Jesus always stressed forgiveness. Repeatedly He taught that we must forgive to be forgiven (Matthew. 6:14, 15; 18:35; Mark 11:25, 26; Luke 6:37; 2 Corinthians. 2:10; John 20:23). John tells us that judgment and unforgiveness will scatter relationships and shatter our inner peace and joy.

Our response to offenses affects our health and well-being more than most of us want to admit. Just the mention of certain names and our backs begin to stiffen. Our minds are flooded with unhappy, angry, bitter, and painful memories. A good day can become a terrible day just by seeing somebody in the grocery store or hearing someone mention a certain name. These offenses are unresolved issues or unforgiven debts.

You cannot be free until you free others. Somehow, the unforgiveness you hold out to others becomes the pain and suffering you inflict upon yourself. Where is the wisdom in this self-inflicted pain because of the wrongdoing of another? Jesus wants us to realize that by releasing others of offense, we are actually freeing ourselves to be happy again.

Forgiveness is a choice--not an emotion. Jesus said we are to forgive seventy times seven for each offense because He understood that it often takes time to overcome the pain. If you will purpose in your heart to love the person who has wronged you, to pray for them, to bless them, and to speak only good about them, your healing process will begin. If you feel you cannot forgive, ask God to do it through you. With God, all things are possible--even loving your enemies. Each time the memory of the offense comes up, choose again to forgive and pray for that person. As you do this day after day, week after week, and month after month, you will begin to recognize the healing process that God is working in you. Do not be discouraged if it takes time, and do not quit forgiving. The freedom you gain will be worth the energy required to walk through the seven natural steps to forgiveness listed below.

Step 1: Nothing happened; nothing is wrong (denial).
Step 2: It is ALL my fault. (If I hadn't done, or If I had done...)
Step 3: They had no right to do that! A-N-G-E-R!
Step 4: I am going to be okay. I still have value.
Step 5: Their problem does not have to become my problem.
Step 6: They have a problem that affects them in many relationships, not just with me.
Step 7: Father, forgive them for they didn't realize what they did to me.

Complete forgiveness is when you care for their souls. You don't have to become their friends, but you need to care about their eternity.

Dear God, Teach me complete forgiveness. I am willing, but I need help.

(These steps were adapted from my personal experiences and hearing seven steps to forgiveness taught from several different perspectives. (Original source unknown.)
CR: Forgiveness, Heart Issues

31 HELP ME TO ESTEEM MY FELLOW TEACHERS!

Philippians 2:3-4 *Do nothing out of selfish ambition or vain conceit, but in humility value others above yourselves, not looking to your own interests but each of you to the interests of the others.*

It is easier to see things from our perspective; our thinking always seems so much more reasonable than the other person's ideas. Philippians adjures us not to seek our own way at the risk of hurting others. We are to avoid strife when possible. We must try to understand and respect others' opinions in order to work as a team.

Easier said than done, huh? You may ask, "Aren't there times that a disagreement is unavoidable? What if the issue involves sinful actions?" The key words are "lowliness of mind." We must stand for what is godly and righteous, but we are also to stand with humility desiring the best for all those involved. We must be considerate of others' opinions even when they are in direct opposition to our own. Learn to check messages to make sure you are communicating accurately. (Is this what you are saying? I understand that you feel...). Do not compromise right for wrong. However, sometimes you can offer creative solutions that do not require you to disobey God. Be friendly in your discussions and allow others to keep their opinions. If you are the authority, you must make the decision when compromise is not possible. If they are your authority, you must submit as long as the action does not cause you to sin. (You must always obey the highest authority.) If you are equals, you may need to work independently if a compromise is not found.

True love *is not self-seeking* (I Corinthians 13:5) and true humility thinks of others' needs. If we truly esteem the other person better than we do ourselves, we consider them #1. If they are serving God and they esteem you as better than themselves, they will consider you #1. If you are #1 in their eyes and they are #1 in your eyes, then there is no #2. This is God's plan for coworkers in His Kingdom. *Blessed are the peacemakers, for they will be called the sons of God* (Matthew 5:9).

Dear God, It is so hard to give up my opinion. Help me to be reasonable. Teach me to listen to someone else's opinion and be willing to learn. Also, help me to communicate clearly, so my ideas can be understood. Above all, teach me humility, submission, and the meaning of true love.

CR: Communications, Love, Coworkers, Authority

32 GIVE ME THE RIGHT WORDS IN TIMES OF CONFLICT

Colossians 4:6 *Let your conversation be always full of grace, seasoned with salt, so that you may know how to answer everyone.*

Sometimes you have "just had it." Your patience wears thin with students who test the boundaries. Students want to know whether you will stand firm or collapse under the pressure of their misbehavior. Classroom rules are essential. If you fail to enforce the rules, you will lose more than a battle; you will lose the students' respect. You cannot afford to give up or give in. Students are more secure when the teacher enforces boundaries.

God is our refuge during these stressful times. Since deep meditation and prayer are not possible, you must depend on the constant abiding presence of the Holy Spirit. A silent, inward cry for help brings the heavens to stand alert. Ask God for help. Do not rely on your own stamina and abilities. God's supernatural wisdom and strength are available to you in an instant. Just ask.

Be slow to speak! Allow yourself time to think before saying or doing anything. Lectures do not work on repeated offenses! Have a plan of action before the conflict. Follow the plan. (Stress often indicates that you have not followed the discipline plan consistently.) You are in charge. Anger is unnecessary! Anger belittles your position and causes you to lose your students' respect. Love the child--correct the behavior. The behavior is not the child; the misbehavior is his childishness! Foolishness is found in the heart of a child, but correction helps set him on the right path again. (Proverbs. 22:15)

Seasoning our words with grace and salt (love and firmness), will eventually help students to understand that you are working "for" them and not against them. Consistent training in self-control will teach students respect and obedience. Most misbehavior will gradually fade with loving correction. Be loving and firm with a serving and caring attitude. Without grace and love, your students may perceive your firmness as a personal attack.

Dear God, I want to control my tongue when students push me too far. When I have to be salt to cleanse the behavior of my students, let it always be for their good and not because I am angry or irritated at them.

CR: Discipline, Tongue, Heart Issues, Anger

33 LET MY LIFE BE A LIGHT TO SOMEONE TODAY

Psalms 119:130 *The unfolding of your words gives light; it gives understanding to the simple.*

At the end of my lesson on being thankful, I said, "Your final assignment for today is to write a letter. The letter can be addressed to anyone—your mother, your friend, your teacher, or someone else. It is due at the end of the period. After I grade it, you may mail or deliver your letter, if you like."

After the bell rang, twenty-five letters lay on my desk. Several students wrote letters to their friends, some wrote to their family members and others to their teachers, but one letter was addressed to me. It was a complete surprise. It was from a boy that I felt I was unable to reach. He was always into mischief. His demeanor said that the things I taught in Bible were of no interest to him. No matter what I tried, I always felt that he had a deaf ear to spiritual things. Then I got his letter (paraphrased).

Dear Mrs. Wyrick,

I know that you love God with all your heart. I can see it when you teach Bible. I know I act like I don't care about God, but I do. Right now, I am having a real bad time in my life. I am not doing right, but I want to do better. Please pray that someday I can learn to love God as much as you do.

I sat quietly in my empty classroom and held the letter in my hand. I read it again, and then a third time. Tears came to my eyes, and a prayer formed in my heart. "Thank you Lord for allowing Your light in me to touch this student. Help him to find you. Help him to know you personally and to love you deeply as he builds a closer relationship with you. Give him good friends that will help lead him in the way he should go. Watch over him as he walks through these difficult times in his life."

When you plant seeds, you never know which seed is going to produce the greatest harvest. Love each student unconditionally. Show concern, kindness, and gentleness to them all. God often chooses the 'least likely' person to join His army.

Dear God, Fill my heart with love and compassion for those struggling with sin. Help me to set your standard of righteousness before them in such a way that they are drawn to your light. May my students see Jesus through my words and my actions

CR: Devotion to God; Love, Heart Issues

34 GIVE ME WISDOM TO MEET THE CHALLENGES

2 Timothy 2:24-26 *And the Lord's servant must not be quarrelsome but must be kind to everyone, able to teach, not resentful.* [25] *Opponents must be gently instructed, in the hope that God will grant them repentance leading them to a knowledge of the truth,* [26] *and that they will come to their senses and escape from the trap of the devil, who has taken them captive to do his will.*

Some topics create heated discussions in a classroom--discussions that cannot be proven, cannot be solved, and will set the classroom at odds. I avoid these topics. There are disagreements within society that will not be solved, and are nonessential to the overall success of the Kingdom of God or my classroom's yearly essential elements. Some students look for a "question" to get you started. Face it, class is more fun if you can get the teacher off the lesson and onto a debate that brings excitement.

As the Lord's servant, we are not to quarrel. If the issue is unbiblical and you can quickly "instruct" the student to further understanding--do it...gently! However, these matters (though they need to be addressed) are usually better dealt with privately after class. If the student's question is genuine, he will appreciate you taking time to answer the question. If the student is trying to stir up a discussion or an argument, he will be disappointed and unexcited about handling the question privately. As you consistently confront his questions after class, he will soon give up his rabbit chases.

At the time of the "off track" question, simply say, "That is an interesting question, but I do not think this is a good time to discuss it. See me after class, and we can talk about it. Now, let us get back to our lesson..." or "I am sorry, but we need to stick with our lesson today. Does someone else have a question that pertains to our lesson?"

Should students try to challenge your knowledge or your authority, do not try to "prove" your qualifications or get into a battle of wits. The student should be confronted privately regarding his inappropriate behavior and informed that his "off-track" questions are disruptive and cannot be allowed. Remember to reprove him gently. If the student should continue this "attack" in the classroom, meet with your principal and develop a specific plan of action to stop his disruptions. Never ignore disrespect or challenges-- gently (but firmly) reprove.

Dear God, Help me to be secure enough as a teacher that I can gently reprove a challenging student without anger or resentment. Teach me to respond as a Christian and a professional teacher.

CR: Discipline, Anger,

35 RENEW ME DURING CHRISTMAS BREAK

Isaiah 40:31 *But they that wait upon the LORD shall renew their strength; they shall mount up with wings as eagles; they shall run, and not be weary; and they shall walk, and not faint (KJV).*

Teachers value their holiday vacations. While preparing for your yearly celebrations, don't forget to rest, refocus and spend quality time with your family and friends. To build joy and a holiday spirit, give time, money, or a gift to someone in need. Perhaps you and your family could visit a nursing home or homeless shelter to bring small gifts to those in need. Seek to show extra kindness to those who work long hours in the department stores to assist you in your purchases. Of course, special thank you notes included in your Christmas cards are always uplifting.

Did you suddenly feel overwhelmed with the responsibility of what you SHOULD or MUST do? All of us know we can get overwhelmed with the things that need to be done. A "sense of duty" can drive you through the holidays and you will find yourself more exhausted than you were before the break. These few days of vacation are valuable times of regrouping and resting. Don't try to do it all--to please everyone, to attend all the parties, and to get all the projects completed. In all your doings, don't forget your quiet times with God. Allow the Word of God to refresh you and bring new perspective to your responsibilities. Wait quietly before the Lord to gain new insight and focus on the race set before you. Allow God to renew your strength, to create in you a new heart and renew in you a right spirit. You will be able to run and not be weary, to walk and not faint.

Dear God, Teach me to prioritize my time this holiday season. Lead me to activities that will renew and strengthen me in my mind, body and spirit. Help me to avoid the traps of trivia so readily available throughout the day.

36 AM I PURSUING GOD OR MY OWN COMFORT?

Deuteronomy 11:16 *Take heed to yourselves, that your heart be not deceived, and ye turn aside, and serve other gods, and worship them.*

Both children and adults search for "heroes" and people of influence to admire, to follow, and to please. People want to belong and to feel accepted by peers. Peer pressure gains control when the desire to "fit in" is stronger than the desire to please God. No one wants to be rejected or be in conflict with the group. In reality, there will be times when those who follow Christ will have to take "The Road Less Traveled" (Robert Frost).

God wants to be first in our lives. This does not mean we have to give up friends and position. Instead, we are to be His hand extended by being a great friend to others and by being a positive influence to the group. This works wonderfully if your group wants to do the right thing. However, if your group is bent on going toward the path that displeases God, you are instantly placed in the crossroad position of having to choose which road you will follow.

Life can be difficult; choices are often unpleasant and stretching. Deuteronomy 11:16 warns us that our heart can be deceived; that we can lose our way and follow other gods without realizing that we have left our path. Remember, as the prodigal son came to his senses, he turned back to his father's house. This is the answer to our wandering. When we begin to see the deceit and error of our ways, we can quickly turn toward our Heavenly Father who understands our wanderings, our gullibility, and our failures. He is waiting to restore us back to the path He designed for us. His love is great and unconditional. He is waiting with open arms to set our hearts right.

Dear God, Create in me a clean heart and renew in me a right spirit. I choose to follow you with an undivided heart.
CR: Discipline, Rebel, Anger

37 TEACH ME TO STAY IN THE BOUNDARIES OF MY JOB

Ecclesiastes 2:24-25 *A person can do nothing better than to eat and drink and find satisfaction in their own toil. This too, I see, is from the hand of God, [25] for without him, who can eat or find enjoyment.*

It amazes me how staff and teachers always have better ideas than administrators and principals do, and how students always have better ideas than teachers do. In fact, it seems that my superiors always made decisions that were unfair, thoughtless, and required too much unnecessary work. Does that sound familiar?

I must admit that I experienced these feelings as a child, as a student, as a secretary, as a teacher, as a principal, and as a school administrator. In fact, I cannot think of any of my jobs where I did not, at one time, experience these feelings of frustration and discontent. However, as I progressed up the "ladder" of leadership, I made a discovery. Decisions always seem much more simple, clear-cut, and obvious to those who do not have to make them than to those who carry the responsibility of leadership.

For instance, a student feels it is a simple thing to dismiss school. “If everyone is tired, then we should just dismiss for a day of rest.” Sounds simple, but leaders know that this is not reasonable. Feelings cannot be our measurement of attendance. Although this seems naive, the decision you are questioning from your authority may be as simple and clear-cut to your boss and not to you.

The basic principle is "know your place.” Know when you have the authority to make a decision, and know when a decision belongs to a higher authority. Do not cross the line. Know the boundaries of your responsibilities and decision-making privileges. Learn to obey directives quickly, quietly and gladly. When you cannot find peace with the decision, prayerfully prepare to make a private appeal to your leader. Offer an alternative solution as you express your concern. Be careful! If you are constantly questioning or appealing your authority's decisions, you will negate the validity of your appeals. In fact, your appeals will probably never be seriously considered. Save your appeals for the important issues. Obey without comment or conflict for the smaller issues. Choose your battles carefully.

Dear God, Teach me to be a good follower. Help me to understand that my boss may be basing decisions on a bigger picture than mine. Give me grace to understand and accept your principles of authority. Teach me satisfaction in my job.

CR: Leadership, Boss, Obedience, Appeal

38 A TERRIBLE, ROTTEN, LOUSY, NO-GOOD DAY

Hebrews 12:1-2 *Therefore, since we are surrounded by such a great cloud of witnesses, let us throw off everything that hinders and the sin that so easily entangles. And let us run with perseverance the race marked out for us, fixing our eyes on Jesus, the pioneer and perfecter of faith. For the joy set before him he endured the cross, scorning its shame, and sat down at the right hand of the throne of God.*

Ever had one of those days? Nothing goes right; everything you touch breaks; everything you say is wrong; all your hopes are shattered; all your friends are mad at you. It's just a terrible, rotten, lousy, no-good day. Hebrews 12:2 gives us a key to overcoming on these days—"looking unto Jesus." Although this statement may seem simplistic or trite, the Bible gives a KEY to a better day.

1. Get alone (even for 5 minutes).
2. Take a deep breath; relax; refocus.
3. Cry out to God for peace and restoration.
4. Meditate on Jesus--who was, is, and is to come.
5. Recite or sing this song:

Turn your eyes upon Jesus.
Look full in His wonderful face,
And the things of earth will grow strangely dim
In the light of God's glory and grace.
(Words & Music by Helen H. Lemmel, 1922)

God is the author of your life and of your faith; He is also the finisher. He, who began a good work in you, will be faithful to complete it (Philippians. 1:6). Jesus endured the cross by looking past the pain to the finished product. We can also look past our current pain and frustration by turning our eyes to greater, eternal purposes. Allow God to restore your joy today by refocusing on the one who made your joy complete--Jesus Christ.

Dear God, Thank you for your son. Thank you for your truth. As I turn my eyes to the truth, allow the truth to set me free so I can find peace in the midst of turmoil.

CR: Heart Issues, Attitude, Truth

39 MAY LOVE DRAW MY STUDENTS TO CHRIST

John 14:23 *Jesus replied, "If anyone loves me, he will obey my teaching. My Father will love him and we will come to Him and make our home with Him."*

I believe the above scripture gives the "key" to developing godly, obedient students who follow Christ. If a student loves Jesus, he will obey him. Perhaps we emphasize the rules more than we tell the story of Jesus. Perhaps, we, as Christians, major on the "laws" and not on the "love" of God. Perhaps, we, in our own personal lives, do not reflect the deep love and excitement toward our Savior that would draw our students to learn at the feet of Jesus.

How do you build devotion and love toward someone? The answer is in knowing them. As teachers, I encourage you to tell the story of Jesus, again, and again, and again. Tell your students of his faithfulness to you and your friends. Help them to see God's involvement in your everyday life. Take prayer requests in your classroom and allow students to bring testimonies of answered prayers. Commit every problem in your classroom to the Lord. Let your walk with God be a public example of loving God and leaning upon Him for your strength and direction. The Light of Jesus they see in your life will draw them to Him.

If you are teaching in a school where you are limited in your testimony, you can still be the light. Let the love of Christ permeate your actions and your words. Pray privately for the needs of your students; be concerned about their needs. Without using words about God or Jesus, students will see the difference in your life and be drawn to you, and God will draw them to Himself. Truth and light make changes in others no matter where they are released.

Dear God, Do me again. Let the flame of love for You be rekindled. Make me a bright light for your kingdom and draw my students to you as I draw closer too. Give me eyes to see the opportunities you provide for me to tell them about Jesus.

CR: Heart Issues, Holy Spirit Guidance, Love

40 BE LED BY THE HOLY SPIRIT

John 16:13 *But when he, the Spirit of truth, comes, he will guide you into all truth. He will not speak on his own; he will speak only what he hears, and he will tell you what is yet to come.*

God, the Creator, designed every student in your classroom. He knows each child personally and knows the details of individual environments and experiences that affect the learning process. When you feel you have run into a brick wall with a student, do not panic. God has the answer for every child. He knows where the door of understanding is, and He is willing to lead you to the "truth" that will set the child free to learn again.

Rather than depend totally upon "techniques and teaching styles," the Christian teacher should always be prepared to rely on the Holy Spirit to lead him/her into truth. Remember, those who seek wisdom will find it. Learn to get quiet before the Lord and ask for His guidance through each difficult task. He is neither unconcerned nor unwilling. Anyone asking for wisdom will receive it. It is the "bread" for those who serve Him.

Pray about everything--schedules, discipline problems, learning difficulties, parent problems, and coworker problems. Share your day minute by minute with the Holy Spirit. He will lead you into all truth.

Dear God, Lead me into your truth. Give me wisdom beyond myself. Show me the secrets of educating my students that only you know.

CR: Holy Spirit Guidance, Wisdom

41 IF IT WEREN'T FOR THE KIDS, I'D HAVE A GOOD DAY

Proverbs 14:4 *Where there are no oxen, the manger is empty, but from the strength of an ox comes an abundant harvest.*

Do you ever have those days that you feel like teaching school would not be so bad if it weren't for the students? Do you ever get tired of the sticky fingers, smudged glass doors, or crumpled book pages? If we're honest, most of us feel that way from time to time. It's not that we don't love our students, but sometimes the effort required to lead and teach them becomes tedious.

This is how I was feeling when I discovered this verse. It was the first fall break of the new school year. As I was cleaning and reorganizing my classroom, I discovered that one of my students had spilled little round hole-punches all over the floor. The mess caused me to remember how tired I was last May. Then the reality that I would face more challenges this year caused me to sit and consider my career. A teacher's job can be demanding even without the messes. Yes, without the kids, teaching would be a great job! Without the children, my classroom would be well organized, clean, and lovely. However, the value of teaching--the reason for my efforts is bundled up in those children. Even as much work as the children require, the hope for tomorrow's world is packaged in those rowdy, sometimes unruly, young boys and girls. I decided it was worth it. I dutifully began to pick up the little round dots.

What a privilege to be called to teach children! They are our investment for a better tomorrow. This realization, alone, is enough to encourage me to again press me toward the high calling set before me. I consider it a privilege to be called "teacher."

Dear God, Thank you for placing me in the classroom to help direct the children toward your truths and your ways. I need your wisdom and guidance daily for such an awesome task.

CR: Heart Issues, Leadership, Attitude

42 LET ME TEACH MY STUDENTS TO HONOR THEIR PARENTS

Ephesians 6:2-3 *"Honor your father and mother"--which is the first commandment with a promise-- [3] "that it may go well with you and that you may enjoy long life on the earth."*

In today's society, many parents do not train their children to honor them. They do not require respect and obedience from family members. Biblically, a child should not address an adult in the same way they address a classmate. Even though this is swimming upstream from modern society, you need to teach this to your class. Role plays and short lessons in respect can reinforce the student's understanding of this principle. They are never too young to understand that they need to learn how to deal with authority. If they don't develop respect for authority, someday, when they fail to respond correctly to their boss, they may lose a job.

You, the teacher, cannot change the training being given at home. However, you can instill truths in the child through short lessons at school. Should parents come for counsel to ask how to help their child at home, or should they mention that their child seems to behave better at school than they do at home, you will have the opportunity to share valuable knowledge about student discipline. The discipline pointers may enable parents to support discipline training at home, which will, hopefully, build better family experiences and relationships.

Do not be afraid of the parents; become their co-workers. They have the student more hours than you do. Any consistency you can establish between the home and the school will be to everyone's advantage.

You may want to have parent days and invite parents to visit the classroom one day during the year. This will help bond the parent to the school. You can honor them as the parents of the day. During their visit, which can be one or two hours long, ask them to share with the class about their jobs and other interesting hobbies they do. You may even want to have seats of honor at the lunch table for the Parents of the Day. A follow-up thank you card would be appropriate.

The more that students understand the honor due to those in authority, the greater unity and discipline you will experience in your classroom.

Dear God, Help me to honor parents--all of them. Forgive me if I have preferred one parent over another. Give me creative ideas on how to show respect and honor to the parents of my students.

CR: Discipline, Parents, Respect, Attitude

43 GRATITUDE IS THE KEY TO JOYFUL SERVICE

2 Corinthians 8:7 *But since you excel in everything—in faith, in speech, in knowledge, in complete earnestness and in the love we have kindled in you—see that you also excel in this grace of giving.*

Do you ever feel that you are carrying the biggest load at school? Or that the other teachers or parents are not doing their part? Do you ever resent having to do the little things that others thoughtlessly leave undone? Have you considered refusing to do your part because others don't seem to do theirs?

One day, when I became frustrated with all the menial tasks I was being asked to do, I made the statement "I'm nothing more than a servant around here!" A Christian man who was walking through the building heard me and stopped to say, "What's wrong with being a servant? Aren't we supposed to be? Jesus was." I ducked my head, smiled and continued with my tasks knowing he had spoken the truth. God offers us the grace to give whether it is time, money, energy, friendship, or love. If we are willing to accept the position of service, God will give us His grace to do what we're asked to do.

In Luke 17:7-9 Jesus explained that a servant should not expect to be thanked for doing his duty. Why was I becoming so angry in my "serving"? The answer jumped out at me--RIGHTS! I was holding on to my rights! I felt others were not doing their part! I had a right to have help. I had a right to expect others to do their part. A servant has no rights; he has responsibilities! I was guilty of "stinking thinking". As I submitted before God, asking him to show me His truth, I admitted the following:

1. I am 100% responsible for my attitude.
2. I only have control over my actions and attitude--no one else's attitude.
3. I can only change me.
4. My unfulfilled expectations of coworkers created anger in me. I was miserable.
5. I could choose to serve them and have no expectations of them.

6. I can be truly grateful should my coworkers pitch in to help. Since I have no expectations of them, I am free to say thank you instead of "It's about time."
7. I have the responsibility to train my students to serve and carry their part, but, as a teacher I have no position to hold my coworkers accountable for their performance.
8. My service is before God; I am not to stop doing my duty because other coworkers are being irresponsible.
9. I am not to become proud because I am doing MY PART.
10. I will not die from doing more than my share, and I can choose to do more than my part when needed.
11. I can show my commitment and love for Jesus Christ by going the second mile.
12. Service is an act of love.

People enjoy serving with someone who has a grateful attitude. We can be grateful to God for all He has given and all he has taught us. God offers the grace of giving to anyone who is willing to receive it.

Dear God, Gratitude is the key. Give me a servant's heart and restore to me the joy of giving. Make me like you, Lord--a servant!

CR: Coworkers, Attitude, Rights, Service, Leadership

44 TEACH ME TO BE GRACIOUS

Colossians 4:6 *Let your conversation be always full of grace, seasoned with salt, so that you may know how to answer everyone.*

How many times have we purposed in our hearts that we are not going to be hateful or backbiting to someone when a certain topic comes up in the conversation? And, what do we do? Yes, we do exactly what we said we would not do! God's Word has some specific directions for each of us in this matter. James 4:6 says, "*God opposes the proud but shows favor to the humble*."

What is humility? Humility is NOT...thinking less of yourself! Humility IS...not thinking of yourself at all! When you are full of grace (seasoned with salt), you are spreading goodness, cheer, and concern for your fellowman. Your words will become a blessing and not a cursing to your brother. After all, isn't that what Jesus taught in Luke 6:28 *Bless those who curse you, pray for those who mistreat you.*

Teachers can create even more conflict by the way they answer a student or a parent in an emotional issue. Purpose in your heart to extend grace to those you serve through gentleness and kindness--even when they are not showing you the grace of Christ. As school teachers, we are the example to be followed. Let Christ dwell within you richly (Colossians. 3:16) and let His light shine through your words (and tone) to reflect his unconditional acceptance even when others are being unlovely. Remember, a soft answer turns away wrath.

Dear God, Give me the strength to empty me of myself enough to learn humility. Teach me to be slow to speak. Give me soft words when I do speak. Fill me with your grace and let it overflow in my daily walk. Let the love of Christ within me cover a multitude of sin in others.

CR: Teacher , Coworkers, Authority, Character, Humility, , Soft Answer, Leadership

45 TEACH ME TO PROPERLY HONOR OTHERS

1 Peter 2:17 *Show proper respect to everyone, love the family of believers, fear God, honor the emperor.*

Does it irritate you when people's opinions are the opposite of your own? Do you get impatient with parents or other teachers who have advice for you that doesn't agree with your ideas? Do you feel frustrated when you are unable to change someone's opinions to match your own?

Learning to respect the other persons' right to think their own thoughts and follow their own ideas is a maturing process that many never master. Each of us tends to believe that we know best! The truth is that we can learn from anyone. Sometimes we learn "how to do something;" sometimes we learn "another way to do something;" and sometimes we learn "how not to do something."

We should seek to be an observer of life and of people. We should inspect each new idea carefully by comparing that idea with the truth in scriptures. If it is not in disagreement with the scriptures, we can be safe to examine the idea further. However, if it does not agree with the Bible, we must recognize it as error and reject it. As Christians, all truth comes from the Word (the Bible). It is our standard--our measuring rod. We must remember to reject only the idea, not the person. God loves each of us, even in our error. Our unconditional love for someone in error may be the key to bringing that person to the truth someday.

All of us can honor an authority's position; respect the person; inspect their ideas; and know the truth. We can remain friendly without forming a friendship. We can honor a position without agreeing with the person. We can esteem the person without accepting their philosophy. They are God's creation and that is enough reason to treat others with respect and consideration.

Dear God, Teach me to mature in the area of esteeming, honoring and respecting others. Sometimes my opinion of others is harsh and judgmental. Teach me to see them through your eyes of love and compassion.

CR: Love, Coworkers, Leadership, Authority, Attitude, Respect

46 HELP ME TO BE TEACHABLE TODAY

Proverbs 4:13 *Hold on to instruction, do not let it go; guard it well, for it is your life.*

Life is a learning process. Beginning teachers learning from the experienced teachers, teachers learning from their principal, the parents learning from the staff, the staff learning from listening to the parents, students learning from teachers, teachers learning from students and students learning from other students. Every conflict has a lesson in it; every success has a truth in it; and every failure has a future purpose.

The key to learning is not just the lesson but, also, the student's willingness to learn. Those who run after wisdom and desire knowledge will soak it up like a sponge. They will learn. Even the worst principal, teacher, parent, or student has something to teach you. Sometimes our greatest lessons are "how not to do something" as we see others fail.

In the above Scripture, there is a sense of urgency. "Hold on..., do not let it go; guard it..." Students need to sense this deep desire for understanding and knowledge in us. They will begin to build a lifestyle of seeking the truth as they begin to pattern their lives after ours. As educators, we must never lay down our quest for truth. New information, new techniques, and new applications are available in conferences, magazines, books, and evening classes. As students of the Word of God, we should approach church services with open hearts to learn more truth. If we become disinterested in sermons or in Bible study, we need to check to see if we have become proud, arrogant, and unteachable. Let us again pick up our paper and pencil to take the position of student—a student of life. If we live long enough, we may even find ourselves learning from those who were once our students. We can learn from anyone. Truth is everywhere for us to grasp. Reach for it.

Dear God, It is my desire to be teachable. There is so much knowledge and understanding needed in today's world. May I never become the unteachable teacher--one who hardens my heart toward you and your truth.

CR: Teachable, Coworkers, Conflict

47 TEACH US TO BE UNIFIED

Hebrews 12:15 *See to it that no one misses the grace of God and that no bitter root grows up to cause trouble and defile many.*

United we stand; divided we fall. Satan will use the "divide and conquer" tactic to destroy friendships and hinder academic progress this year. God's grace and forgiveness are our weapons for this battle.

Why do people have so much trouble living in unity? We think differently; we were raised in different environments, cultures, economic classes, and religious backgrounds. We have different priorities and values. Some teachers still have difficulties with personal insecurity, and become too emotionally entangled in conflicts. And, others just don't like to yield or admit error. In spite of all these differences, we can have peace through love, acceptance, and forgiveness.

Resolving differences must be a priority for each teacher. As administrators and teachers, we must find the grace of God in our hearts to actively pursue peace. We should seek to restore any parent or student who is at odds with the school, when possible. We do this by going to the person(s) involved and talking about the offense. Ignoring the offense will not make it go away. But talking about the problem to those involved often resolves the conflict and brings peace.

Search daily for any root of bitterness that may be trying to form in your school. Satan is sly. He comes in like a wolf in sheep's clothing. He will defile us if we do not daily search for wrong attitudes and work to bring healing to wounded hearts.

Dear God, teach me to be a peacemaker. Help me to understand the importance of unity and my responsibility as a teacher to keep conflicts out of the school. I realize that only the Grace of God can give me what I need to handle some of the conflicts that I have to deal with this year. Heavenly Father, I need your grace today.

CR: Forgiveness, Anger, Conflict, Coworkers, Attitude, Unity, Grace

48 HELP ME TO OBEY MY SUPERVISOR

Hebrews 13:17 *Have confidence in your leaders and submit to their authority, because they keep watch over you as those who must give an account. Do this so that their work will be a joy, not a burden, for that would be of no benefit to you.*

Do you ever feel that your ideas are better than your principal's decisions? Do you ever feel that you could run the school better than he/she does? Do you ever find yourself speaking against your leaders to other coworkers and disagreeing with their leadership? Do you ever do a procedure different from your instructions because you feel your way is better or it doesn't really matter? If so, the above scripture is addressed to you.

Giving up our own will to follow a leader's directives is a difficult but necessary lesson. Submission is God's way.

Obedience is God's way. If God sets leaders in place, (Romans 13:1), then He gave you that leader to follow. When you follow that leader, you are following Christ. God exalts good followers who become good leaders. Leaders who have never followed are overbearing and thoughtless of their workers. Learn to obey, even unkind "masters", and you will build godly character that will exalt you in position later. Remember, God orders your steps; therefore, you are assigned the task of learning to follow this leader!

When do you obey, and when do you refuse to obey? You obey until a higher authority gives different instructions. In other words, if it is not against God's law, if it is not against the laws of the land, and if it is not against company policy, then you are to obey. An employer pays your salary. That gives them the privilege to decide how you spend your time on the job. They pay you to do what they ask you to do. It is your job to give them what they want (within the above laws). You can offer a creative idea as an alternative, but if they don't accept your idea, don't get mad. Leading the school is their job. They will carry the ultimate responsibility of success or failure. Simply obey. Obey gladly unto the Lord knowing that you are pleasing God by obeying your leaders.

Dear God, I want to learn obedience. Doing my job differently than I think it should be done is a difficult thing for me. Sometimes I get concerned that things are not "fair". Help me to give up my "rights" and take on obedience. I want to please you. Make me a servant like your son, Jesus Christ.

CR: Character Traits, Authority, Obedience, Appeal, Boss

49 TEACH ME TO GLORIFY GOD IN MY SUCCESS

Psalms 75:6-7 No one from the east or the west or from the desert can exalt themselves. [7] But it is God who judges: He brings one down, he exalts another."

Many men start their leadership role with the right goals and attitudes. They have good and just intentions. But, as time passes, their purposes blur and selfish ambition, greed, pride, rebellion, and other areas of sin begin to manifest. Why does this happen?

A leader's greatest success can be his greatest stumbling block for the future. Rewards and praise can bring over-confidence and self-sufficiency. Does that mean that we are never to praise or reward one another? No! But it does mean that we, as leaders, must be aware of the tendency to fail after experiencing success. Too many leaders tend to separate themselves from the people we have been asked to lead. Subordinates find it increasingly difficult to get an appointment. To affect the lives of those we lead, we must be available to them. If we are not careful, we will lose sight of our goals. We must daily remind ourselves that the Holy Spirit living within us is the creative force behind our success. We must choose to give God the glory for all things and continue to walk in lowliness of mind—in humility (not thinking of ourselves at all). (Philippians 2:3-4) Your success is from God. You will remain successful only as long as He wills it. Your response to success determines whether God can trust you with even greater success. Your leadership will either earn you more responsibility or cause you to lose position. God exalts and God demotes. Your response to those you lead and to your daily duties will affect future promotions.

Matthew 23:11-12 says, *The greatest among you will be your servant. [12] For those who exalt themselves will be humbled, and those who humble themselves will be exalted.*

Humble yourself before God. Strive to serve the needs of those you lead. God will promote you in due season.

Dear God, Help me to keep my focus and priorities on you and your purposes. May the success you allow me to experience bring greater humility and recognition of the significance of who you are—the creator of all things, the all-knowing, all-present and all-powerful God of the universe. And, help me to remember who I am—a foolish thing (1 Corinthians 1:27) and a sheep that must have a shepherd at all times (1 Peter 2:25).

CR: Leadership, Authority, Boss, Obedience, Attitude, Humility

50 TEACH ME TO DEAL WITH MY ANGER

Ephesians 4:26-27 *"In your anger do not sin": Do not let the sun go down while you are still angry, [27]and do not give the devil a foothold.*

Christians sometimes feel that the best way to respond to anger is pretend that nothing was said or done (denial). We internalize the pain and anger thinking that we have forgiven by turning the other cheek. As we "walk in our forgiveness", the weight of the stuffed anger becomes greater and greater. We may not consciously realize that we are angry. Often we put on masks and pretend the offenses are "forgiven" rather than walking through the full process of letting the offense go completely. The anger we stuff throughout the months and years becomes a boiling pot of unresolved issues that will surface again somewhere. It may surface through poor health, depression (which is often defined as repressed anger), poor relationships, misplaced anger, or God issues like the inability to pray, worship, trust or serve God or others.

The only way to rise above this "stuffed" anger is to begin dealing with each issue. Every wound needs to be addressed. The offenses need to be opened up enough to let the infection drain out. We can ask God to help cleanse us of offenses and to gently bring before us the unresolved issues in the order that we need to forgive. A godly counselor or pastor may be needed for major offenses. As we deal with these stuffed offenses, the Holy Spirit can bring complete healing to the deepest wounds. You may need to go to someone to seek reconciliation with some offenses, while other issues can be privately dealt with in your own heart. As you seek the Lord regarding your offense, the Holy Spirit will guide you to the correct way to deal with each issue.

"Don't let the sun go down upon your wrath" (Ephesians 4:26 KJV). When offended, begin to deal with the issue immediately. The shorter your accounts, the healthier your emotions will become. Loving confrontation can bring healing to both parties.

When I am offended, I have learned to assume that there is a misunderstanding. I also choose to wait until my emotions are under control before I deal with issues. I want to make sure that I do not "offend" as I am seeking my own healing. Two wrongs do not make a right. When I do confront, I begin with an affirmation and proceed with a question regarding the offense. I want to make sure it is not a misunderstanding on my part. I use "I" statements--"I feel ..." rather than "You did ..." This is less attacking. Oh, yes, make sure the confrontation is private. If you need support, your principal, pastor, counselor, or another authority would be appropriate. Your authority should only offer insight and support when needed. You should conduct the conference.

Dear God, Teach me the art of clearing offenses. Help me to become vulnerable enough to confront those who offend me to enable my offender and me to grow more like you. Show me when I am stuffing my anger.

CR: Forgiveness, Anger, Conflict, Holy Spirit Guidance

51 BE A TRUTHFUL LEADER

Ephesians 6:11, 14 *Put on the full armor of God so that you can take your stand against the devil's schemes. . . . [14] Stand firm then, with the belt of truth buckled around your waist...*

Satan plans to trap you today, but the "belt of truth" will protect you. Although telling the truth requires you to be vulnerable and transparent—sometimes completely exposing who you really are or what you actually did, it is your first line of defense.

Students can see through facades. When you are wrong—say so. If you don't know something, admit it and commit yourself to learn it. When you forget something, accept responsibility. Should you respond unkindly, apologize. Where you are irresponsible, admit it and become responsible again. If you lose your temper, repent to those you attacked. It may be difficult to do this at first, but students will have greater respect for you when you are honest about your mistakes.

Our natural response is to hide the real "me" by skirting the truth. We believe people will not accept us as we really are so we develop a "fake" person to present to coworkers, business associates, parents, and students. But Jesus tells us that the truth sets us free to be accepted for who we are and to live honestly, without fear, before God and man. Rather than covering ourselves with facades, let us become transparent before God and man. Choose freedom from performance— freedom from masks and deceptions. Do not be caught in the trap of "doing" just to please others. Confessing your faults sets you free to become someone better than you were (John 8:32).

Dear God, I want to be truthful in all things, in all ways, at all times. Teach me to be as truthful as I want my students to be. Prick my conscience when I am tempted to say anything less than the truth.

CR: Truth, Leadership, Humility

52 MAKE ME A SERVANT LIKE JESUS

Philippians 2:3-4 *Do nothing out of selfish ambition or vain conceit; but in humility, value others above yourselves, [4] not looking to your own interests but each of you to the interests of the others.*

Be ambitious to be nothing! At least nothing except what God designed you to be. When you gave your life to Christ, you became a servant. A servant goes where he is directed and does what he is commanded to do. He takes no thought of whether he "likes" it or not; he simply obeys because of his position. Jesus Christ is our greatest example of a servant. Philippians 2:6-8 tells us how Jesus, who is God, did not try to grasp being equal with God, but made himself to be nothing and became a servant in the form of a man. He became completely submitted and obedient to God, the Father, and submitted even to death on a cross.

There is something in each of us that recoils and wants to strike back when we hear the words servant and submission. We want to say, "I'm a King's kid!" But when searching The Bible we find over and over again that those who exalt themselves will be abased and those who choose to humble themselves before God will be exalted (Matthew 23:12). Remember, God's ways are not our ways; His ways are higher than our ways (Isaiah 55:9).

As we become willing to submit our lives as living sacrifices before God, going where He leads, speaking what He directs, and doing as He asks, the light of God within us will become so evident to those around us that they will want to know what makes us different. Why? Because, it is such an unusual way to live. It has an appeal to those wanting out of the darkness. Your coworkers, parents, and students have a need to see Jesus in you. They will be drawn to the light of Christ as you shine for Him in this dark, confusing world.

Dear God, make me a servant. Jesus was a servant, make me one too. You have placed my students and their parents in my world this year for a reason. Let my light so shine before them that you might be glorified.

CR: Rights, Coworkers, Attitude, Service, Humility

53 MULTITUDES IN THE VALLEY OF DECISION

Joel 3:14 *Multitudes, multitudes in the valley of decision! For the day of the LORD is near in the valley of decision.*

Isaiah 6:8 *Then I heard the voice of the Lord saying, "Whom shall I send? And who will go for us?" And I said, "Here am I. Send me!"*

We do not lead our students to Christ by words alone. As we draw closer to God, the light of Christ will shine from our daily walk, and our students will be drawn to that light. We will win them to Christ as God's love changes our lives, our words, and our deeds. They will see the difference in us and want to follow—at least those who have entered the "Valley of Decision".

Be prepared to lead your students to Christ. Keep a gospel tract or bookmark handy for quick scripture references. Your highest calling as a Christian is to lead others to Christ. Don't hesitate to ask a student (especially when there is difficulty in his life) where he is with God. Ask him how he is getting along with God. Students are often serious and honest in answering this question. Don't be embarrassed to ask. They may be wishing someone would confront them with their need for salvation or a recommitment to God. Many opportunities for prayer and salvation have come when I have asked these questions. Avoid being overly aggressive, rather, let the discussion of spiritual matters be a natural flow from the conversation in progress.

For those who teach in a secular setting, you can teach Bible truths without using scripture and verse. Truth can and should be taught anywhere. Christian character can be taught without using the "Christian" label. Hold the light of God's truth out to your students when possible. You may want to refer them to a local pastor or counselor when possible.

The harvest is ready; many are searching for truth. Will you bring the light to them? Make a commitment to be prepared and willing to lead those in the "Valley of Decision" to the foot of the cross.

Dear God, I want to always be prepared to lead my students in the sinner's prayer. Give me eyes to see those who are ready to hear your salvation message. And may I be willing to say, "Here am I, Lord, use me."

CR: Leadership, Character Traits, Salvation

54 INSTRUCT ME IN YOUR WAYS

Psalms 32:8 *I will instruct you and teach you in the way you should go; I will counsel you and watch over you.*

Thirty-two students filed in to my third period English class. They were talkative and preoccupied as they took their seats. One young lady toward the back of the class continued to be distracted even after I called the class to order and the other students were on task. I asked her to settle down. In response, she retorted some crude and disrespectful statement. I was shocked. Immediately I told her, "You need to see me after class!" She nodded her head and became quiet. I continued with my lessons and the incident was temporarily dropped.

After class, she approached my desk. I was prepared to "let her have it" with a lecture on respect plus assign her consequences that would teach her to never talk to me that way again. But, as she came toward me, the Holy Spirit spoke in that still small voice saying, "Love her. She's hurting. Don't be harsh with her." I instantly changed my approach.

"Honey, what's wrong? That's not like you? What happened?" I asked. She burst into tears and began to explain how she had experienced major humiliation in the class just before mine. She was upset when she came into my classroom, and she took her frustration out on me. She tearfully apologized. She let me know how much she liked me as a teacher, and how she felt bad that she said the things she did. I patted her arm and assured her that I understood. We discussed her embarrassing incident, and I was able to give her some counsel and pray with her.

I never had another disrespectful word from her. Had I not listened to that small "inner" voice of God that was instructing me for that situation, I could have built a wall between us for the entire year. Instead, I was able to love her to correction and help her deal with a difficult experience. Learn to listen carefully. It may transform your relationship with a student as you allow Christ to love them through you.

Dear God, Thank you for your faithfulness and your instruction. You care about my day and you have promised to lead me if I will listen, watch and follow.
CR: Holy Spirit Guidance; Discipline, Restoration

55 ANOINTED TO TEACH

1 John 2:27 *As for you, the anointing you received from him remains in you, and you do not need anyone to teach you. But as his anointing teaches you about all things and as that anointing is real, not counterfeit--just as it has taught you, remain in him.*

Christian teachers are called by God and equipped to teach by His anointing (Holy Spirit empowerment). As a believer in Jesus Christ, you have the Holy Spirit dwelling within you ready and willing to lead you into all truth. In John 16:13 we read that the Holy Spirit will be your guide. You never enter your classroom alone. God's Spirit goes before you to prepare the way and dwells within you to lead you minute by minute (Deuteronomy 31:8). Unfortunately, this truth has not become a living reality for many teachers. Too many teachers still try to separate their "jobs" from their faith. They lean on man's knowledge and fail to include God's supernatural wisdom.

God's Spirit, who has all knowledge and understanding, waits for you to ask for his assistance

(Matthew 7:7-8; James 1:5-7). He holds the "keys" to unlock learning for your students. With His help, you can discern the students' root problems in their educational and behavioral struggles. You can receive creative and unusual ideas for problem solving. He has promised to be your "ever-present help" in your time of need (Psalms 46:1; Hebrews 4:16). Just ask and believe; with God all things are possible.

Learn to rely on God's anointing. During times of stress or decisions, silently cry out to God for guidance. He knows even your "far away" thoughts (Psalms 139:2). You can walk into any situation with confidence if you will rely on God's Spirit to lead you. In God, there is no conflict too great or too stressful for you to handle. You have the counselor of counselors by your side ready to advise you if you will just ask for help.

God desires to give you, as a believer, his direction for today. His still small voice will be there to instruct you about all things. Learn to be sensitive to His leading. Pray for the wisdom to walk in the anointing that God has for you and to hear his direction for today.

Dear God, Guide my thoughts and decisions throughout this week. Open my spiritual ears to hear your still small voice. Teach me your ways and give me the wisdom to follow your direction in my classroom.

56 GO AND MAKE DISCIPLES

Matthew 28:19 *Therefore go and make disciples of all nations ... [20] and teaching them to obey everything I have commanded you...*

As a teen, I feared that God would call me to be a missionary to Africa where I would be forced to eat monkey meat and wormy rice. In my twenties, as I grew closer to God, I committed my entire life to Him. I told God that I would even go to Africa if that was His will for my life. Well, He didn't send me to Africa—at least He hasn't yet.

I told this story to my Bible class using it as an illustration of committing your life completely to Christ. I explained how I became willing to do anything for Christ when I understood that He only does good in my life. As I matured, I realized that doing God's will would bring me the greatest contentment even if it meant going to Africa. I explained to my students that they could trust God to direct their lives.

A young teen attended my Bible classes from grades seven through twelve. Her love for the Lord was obvious, and I knew that God had great plans for her life. After her graduation she entered Bible college and took several missionary trips overseas. After one of her trips, she met with me to share the exciting things happening in her life. She had visited several countries and taught about Jesus. And then she said, "Mrs. Wyrick, remember how you said you were willing to go to Africa if God wanted you to go? Well, you went to Africa." I looked at her puzzled. "You went to Africa through me," she explained. "I taught all the things you taught me in Bible class. I could hear your words coming through me as I taught. So, God really did send you to Africa! I just went for you." The truth of her statement astounded me. Luke 6:40 reminds us that a student . . . *who is fully trained will be like his teacher.*

It is your Great Commission. You are to go into your world, your classrooms, and make disciples of your students. Teach them to obey God's truth and ... *let your light shine before others, that they may see your good deeds and glorify your Father in heaven (*Matthew 5:16). The things you plant into your student's heart will sprout and bring a harvest in God's timing. Don't ever be weary in well doing (Galatians 6:7-9).

Dear God, Thank you for the opportunity to teach children. Keep me humble and near to you at all times so I can reflect your light. May I follow you close enough that others will want to follow you too.

CR: Devotion to God, Leadership

57 DELIVER ME FROM MY RAIN CLOUD

1 Corinthians 4:12-*13 We work hard with our own hands. When we are cursed, we bless; when we are persecuted, we endure it;* [13] *when we are slandered, we answer kindly...*

Being pleasant is not difficult when things go your way, but have you learned to shine during rainy weather? Have you died to your flesh enough to bless when you are cursed, to answer kindly when you are slandered or to endure quietly when you are persecuted?

You only have control over yourself. If you wait for others to treat you right or for things to go better before you have a good attitude, you are giving up your control to someone else. This is a victim's approach to life. A victim feels powerless; they hopelessly wait for someone to change before they can find happiness. But, being happy is a choice. You must take control of your feelings and your behavior if you are going to find peace and contentment.

In Genesis 37, Joseph's brothers sold him into slavery. Joseph's trials were just beginning. He suffered through betrayal, false accusation, and neglect, but Joseph did not sit back and feel sorry for himself. He made the best of each situation he faced. He became the "sunshine" in the dreary prisons. He knew how to choose happiness rather than remain a victim. Joseph knew his God, and he trusted God to always lead his steps for good. This ability to overcome brought him recognition, promotion and success in the middle of the bad situations. And, in God's time, he was promoted out of the pit into the palace.

Learn to act rather than react to life. Make choices—purposeful choices that will bless and not curse others. Do not give your power away by allowing others to steal your peace and joy with their bad attitudes. Remember that the other guy is the one with the problem, not you; therefore, choose to keep your good attitude in spite of his words or actions. With God's help and your commitment to do things His way, you can find sunshine in your life today.

Dear God, None of us like to be falsely accused, slandered or mistreated. I know you want me to be kind, gentle and good even when others do me wrong. I invite your Holy Spirit to do that work in me. Teach me how to choose sunshine instead of rain.

CR: Attitude, Anger, Conflict, Grace

58 HELP ME BE A SACRIFICE FOR YOU!

Romans 12:1 *Therefore, I urge you, brothers and sisters, in view of God's mercy, to offer your bodies as a living sacrifice, holy and pleasing to God—this is your true and proper worship.*

Behold the Lamb that was slain. Jesus was the sacrifice of God! Sacrifices die. They bleed. However, in the verse above, Paul is referring to a different kind of sacrifice. He wants you to be a living sacrifice. Your body continues to live, but you live as a dead man. You are to have no will but the will of God--no mind but the mind of Christ--no emotions but the love of God that blesses and does not curse.

`Your sacrifice is to be offered up to God for the benefit of mankind. You go to your job for the profit of those you serve, not for your own gain. You are a servant, and you are there to serve the needs of others. You don't get angry about being asked to work. That is why you have the job. Let all that you do and say be done for the glory of God.

As we serve our fellow man, we are to be prepared to give an answer—a soft answer (Proverbs 15:1). A soft answer allows you to turn an unreasonable foe into a friend. As you sacrifice your right to be respected and treated correctly, your right to answer back defensively or any other right you may feel you have, you will gain the self-control necessary to represent Christ with a "soft answer". "Soft answers" can bring the unreasonable parent, student or coworker back to being reasonable and able to hear what you are saying. An apology may follow, but do not expect one as your "right". You must forgive their outburst regardless of their willingness to deal with issues in a mature fashion. You are the professional; strive to always respond professionally and like Christ—as a living sacrifice acceptable unto God.

Dear God, This is a hard thing that you ask of me. I do not like to be mistreated; in fact, it makes me angry. Give me the ability to understand your ways of dealing with personal attack. Teach me to be more like you. And when attack comes, please come to my aid quickly. Give me the soft answer that will bring the situation back into control. God, I really need your help on this one.

CR: Leadership, Serve, Sacrifice, Soft Answer

59 SERVANT LEADERS ARE SHEPHERDS

Matthew 20:26-28 *Not so with you. Instead, whoever wants to become great among you must be your servant,* 27 *and whoever wants to be first must be your slave—* 28 *just as the Son of Man did not come to be served, but to serve, and to give his life as a ransom for many.*

Too often teachers figuratively stand at the top of their educational pinnacle looking down on their students, saying "Climb up to my level—stretch, grab hold and climb the mountain. Those who can make it, I will reward with good grades. Those who can't, you will just have to try harder next time or you will never make it. It's up to you."

Jesus said that the greatest teacher would be a servant. A servant-teacher shepherds students. The teacher encourages each one, allows those who can to climb independently, but assists those who are unable to do it alone. A servant-teacher never allows any student to feel alone or unsupported in the climb. A servant-teacher also realizes that some students will climb more naturally than others will. In fact, the teacher may need to come down the mountain to meet the failing student where he/she is. The teacher willingly gives extra time to review the basics of mountain climbing with the faltering student in hopes that he/she will learn the skills and begin the climb to the top. A servant-teacher anticipates the growth and development of all of her students. Not all students will reach the top at the same time, but the desire is to see every student become proficient in climbing and finish the climb. A servant-teacher gives to the students according to their personal needs. Each student's needs are considered individually the same way God deals with each of His children uniquely.

Only God can give you the creativity and sensitivity to be a servant-leader that shepherds your students. Ask Him for guidance and a willing heart to serve.

Dear God, I do care about all of my students. Give me the sensitivity and creativity to see the needs of my students and the courage and fortitude to minister to each individual in my classes.

CR: Serve, Education, and Attitude

60 TEACH ME TO RESTORE AS I DISCIPLINE

Galatians 6:1 ... *if someone is caught in a sin, you who live by the Spirit should restore that person gently.*

Discipline without restoration leads to bitterness and long-term malice. Students are children. Even eleventh and twelfth graders are kids in large bodies. They think like a child and act like a child.

Discipline should direct students to the right path. When the teacher explains the correct response and appropriate attitude for a particular situation, students begin to understand right from wrong. They learn from our patient instructions and our consistent examples. However, unless our own actions portray maturity and grace, we will negate the words we teach by what we do. Our actions will speak louder than our words!

Love must permeate our speech as we correct our students. We must discipline "for" them--not for ourselves. When this is true, we will never allow anger to rule in our hearts. We will understand that the student's actions were not against us, but against the position of authority that we represent. Defend that position with actions not with anger.

Once the consequence of discipline has been discussed and administered (whether it is loss of privilege, instruction, or some other form of correction) it is time to restore the child. Restoration can usually come quickly by reaffirming the child--"Johnny, I care about you and about your future. I know that you want to do better, and, with God's help, you will. Let's get back to the classroom and get on with our work. Okay?" The greatest message that can be given to a person who has messed up is -- You are still okay; everything's back to normal; let's try again; I am not mad at you. A smile, a pat on the back, asking the student to do something for you during the class period, or asking him a question during class discussion assures the student that everything is back to normal.

Dear God, Help me to always restore my students--not just to right action but also to right attitude. Prick my heart when my attitude becomes vindictive instead of loving toward the offender. May I never drive my students to bitterness and resentment.

CR: Discipline, Anger, Restoration

61 REST FOR THE WEARY

Matthew 11:28-30 *Come to me, all you who are weary and burdened, and I will give you rest. 29Take my yoke upon you and learn from me, for I am gentle and humble in heart, and you will find rest for your souls. 30For my yoke is easy and my burden is light.*

When the cares of the world press in on you, and you feel you do not have the strength to teach, stop a few minutes and talk to God. There is no problem too great or too complex that God cannot bring a solution. Rest comes when we become as a little child and trust God.

A master teacher has learned to put aside personal problems and take on the responsibility and concerns of the classroom. With God's help and your understanding of Jesus' words in Matthew 11, you can enter your classroom peacefully and confidently even when your personal life is unsettled.

In reality, only God is big enough to solve your difficulties. Not one minute of worry can change your situation. Not one minute of fretting can protect someone you love. Not one minute of regret can change what happened yesterday. The only answer is your ability to exchange "burdens" with Christ. Leave your burden at the cross and pick up His burden (the work of the Kingdom). Rest comes through trust. There is no other way. It begins with a decision--an act of your will, but it is completed by the power of an Almighty Creator who is touched by your feelings of pain. He is concerned, and in His time He can, and will, make all things beautiful. You can rest through prayer, praise, and trust.

Dear God, Please help me to trust you more. I roll all of my burdens on you today. Take care of them as I set my thoughts and actions toward the task of teaching. I choose to trust you. I will not be afraid, or dismayed.

CR: Conflict, Attitude, Grace, Rest

62 CORRECTION VERSUS PUNISHMENT

1 Peter 3:9 *Do not repay evil with evil or insult with insult, but with blessing, because to this you were called so that you may inherit a blessing.*

When correcting, restoration is our ultimate goal whether we are dealing with students, a fellow teacher, a parent or our own children. Punishment just for the sake of punishment becomes vengeance. Teachers must respond to students with "purpose" rather than "anger".

Loving correction often includes consequences, but the ultimate goal is not the punishment but rather the corrected attitude and behavior. A leader's wrong attitude in the process of correction may stop the outward offense but will embitter the child inwardly and reinforce his determination to be independent of our leadership. Matthew 15:19 tells us that a man's thoughts rule his actions. In major offenses or continually repeated disobedience, students can best be corrected by including a time-out period with individual instruction and introspection to bring new understanding and insight into the motivation behind his misbehavior. If this is done with love and true concern for the child's future--not just punishment--leaders will often see a heart change and growth in maturity.

The student's offense was not against you, personally; a student's misbehavior is against the position you hold. It is not until you, the person, offend him that it becomes a personal issue. The student will not know the difference; but you, the teacher, must understand this to keep your emotions out of the conflict.

Do not repay evil for evil, but rather bless students with your concern for their future. Help them to see how misbehavior affects their lives. A future job may be lost, a marriage may break up, or an arrest may happen if the behavior continues into adulthood. Love the child by leading him/her to correct behavior and self-discipline.

Dear God, Help me to be mature enough to love the unlovely child, to see past his immaturity and rebellion into his future. Help me to correct him, in love, for his future; I want to bless and not curse.

CR: Discipline, Anger, Conflict, Restoration, Love, Immaturity

63 JUSTICE AND MERCY

James 2:13 *...because judgment without mercy will be shown to anyone who has not been merciful. Mercy triumphs over judgment!*

Your success or failure will depend on your classroom discipline. Students cannot learn well in a classroom that is out of control; therefore, control is as much a part of your teaching as the daily lesson plan. A student with knowledge but no self-discipline will not be prepared for the adult world. Each teacher must establish control within the classroom. No principal can do that for you. Written rules of conduct and consequences are essential. Never make the rules up as you go! When students and teachers know the rules and consequences, they can follow the plan with a greater sense of fairness.

The discipline in your classroom must be delicately balanced. There are times that strong correction is needed and other times instruction and mercy are more appropriate. You need to evaluate each situation. Be sensitive to the Holy Spirit. Search for possible explanations of inner motives. You may discover an underlying reason for the student's misbehavior. The student may be experiencing family problems, the dog may have been killed, a friend may have been unkind, anger may be misplaced, or immaturity rather than rebellion may be the issue. Discipline rebellion and train immaturity

Justice should not always reign--sometimes mercy is more humane and more Christ-like. Even as Christ showed you mercy, you can decide to show mercy. A case in point would be a student who earned five detentions because of multiple responses to one incident. This would punish the student for a two-week period. Instead, the student might receive one detention and a three-page essay assignment explaining the importance of obeying the rules (plus a trip to the counselor). Balance is the key to successful discipline. When will we know that our discipline is successful? When the student returns to the class and willingly follows our leadership.

In most situations, follow the rules and hold the line firm. Nevertheless, there are times when mercy is more appropriate than justice. Teachers are to be builders of lives. We must use our discipline decisions as tools to build students toward a better tomorrow. Which--mercy or justice--will train my student for their future? Seek to build better citizens, rather than create bitter students. Remember, discipline is always FOR the student and never AGAINST the student.

Dear God, Teach me balance. Thank you for the mercy you have shown me in my life when I failed. Teach me to recognize my students' need for justice and mercy. Give me the wisdom to appropriately respond in each discipline

situation I encounter. Fill my heart with love for each of my students--especially the one that gives me so much trouble.

CR: Mercy, Discipline, Holy Spirit Guidance, Love

64 AS LONG AS THERE IS LIFE, THERE IS HOPE AND VALUE

Ecclesiastes 9:4 *Anyone who is among the living has hope--even a live dog is better off than a dead lion!*

Do you ever feel that there is no hope for you or possibly no hope for one of your students? This Bible reminds us that where there is life, there is hope. As we grow older, we often realize that our productive classroom years are fading. Our accomplishments seem so small; we wish we had done more. Sometimes we feel that we have wasted our best years just spinning our wheels. The students we did not reach, and the students who never cared seem to haunt our memories. Our victories seem insignificant. STOP! LISTEN! As long as there is life "It ain"t over."

God grants life for a "purpose". He has purpose for your existence. Your place of employment and/or job assignment may change through the years, but you will always have a "purpose". We need to discover God's purpose in each day and pursue it with all our might. Too often we seek the "big picture" before we begin the puzzle. But often God asks us to place each piece of our puzzle before Him daily and He will bring the big picture into focus in His time.

Only God knows who the lions will be. His purposes are valued differently than man values things. Let the Word of God dwell in you richly. Turn from your self-centered thinking to God-centered thinking and leave the final results to God. Set God's work and His love as your goal and press toward it with all your might. Only in eternity will you know how valuable yesterday was in His Kingdom and what today's plans will accomplish. Live today to its fullest. The secret to success is purpose and perseverance. God will lead you if you will follow.

Dear God, Help me to persevere. I choose to not be weary in well doing. I will run the race with patience. Thank you for life and purpose. Lead me down your good path planned for me (Psalms. 16:11; 27:11).

CR: Leadership, Attitude, Education

65 SET A GUARD OVER MY TONGUE

Proverbs 25:2 *It is the glory of God to conceal a matter; to search out a matter is the glory of kings.*

Proverbs 10:12 *Hatred stirs up dissension, but love covers over all wrongs.*

Gossip is fun! If it weren't, it would not trap people. Soap operas play on people's desire to get the latest "scoop". We get hooked into watching the continuing stories. We don't want to miss the latest trauma or victory. We not only want to hear about new developments, but we also want to discuss it with our neighbors and give them our opinion of what's happening. It is a clever way to use a perpetual "story" to build patterns of gossip and judgment in our lives.

During the school year, teachers, parents, students and administrators work closely together. Our strengths and weaknesses become evident. (We all have them!) It pleases God for us to choose to conceal or protect our brother's weaknesses from exposure rather than to make that difficulty a point of conversation. In Matthew 18, we are instructed to go to our brother and him alone to discuss such a matter. The weakness does not have to be a sin issue; it could be an irritating habit or oddity. Damaging slurs toward parents, teachers, or students can infect the entire school climate. A negative statement could be something as simple as "I don't like the way that teacher talks to the students on the playground." Or, it could be in the form of a question, "Do you think he might not being telling all he knows?"

Peace should always be our goal. Remember, slander is a hindrance to your Christian walk. Slander can be defined as "causing someone to think less of someone else." I think Thumper, the little rabbit in the Walt Disney movie, *BAMBI*, had the best idea--"If you can't say something nice, don't say nuttin' at all!"

People leave jobs, schools, and churches as a result of gossip. Even when a bad report is true, the report can create disappointment and disillusionment among the younger members and can harm the entire workplace. It is easy to recognize the damage that careless words bring after the fact, but avoiding the harm is our calling. It is usually beneficial and appropriate for the matter to be handled privately. As a staff, your school can agree to refuse to repeat gossip in the teacher's lounge, hallways, and lunchroom. Avoiding gossip takes effort; it takes a commitment. Self-control will be easier if we can remember that God's love covers a multitude of errors. "[6]*Love does not delight in evil but rejoices with the truth.* [7]*It always protects, always trusts, always hopes, always perseveres.*" (1 Corinthians 13:6-7).

This also applies to the classroom setting. When a student is being disciplined, the issue should remain between the child and the teacher. Discipline is always for the purpose of training the student. We, as school leaders, must never bring harm to the student's social standing. Restoration is our goal. This is what pleases God. Revealing details of an offense is the desire of man, but God's desire is to protect and restore.

Dear God, Make me sensitive as I discipline my students and as I observe the struggles of my coworkers. May I never be anxious to reveal someone's weaknesses. Should I desire to become involved in gossip, quickly reprimand me. Tug on my heart and remind me to seek the glory of God rather than the glory of man.

CR: Discipline, Slander, Gossip, Tongue, Love, Coworkers

66 TEACH ME TO CORRECT NOT JUST PUNISH

Matthew 18:6-7 *But if anyone causes one of these little ones who believe in me to sin, it would be better for him to have a large millstone hung around his neck and to be drowned in the depths of the sea.* [7]*"Woe to the world because of the things that cause people to sin! Such things must come, but woe to the person through whom they come!*

We have the ability to bless or curse our students this year. Our words, actions and attitudes will build-up or tear down their self-worth, their desire to learn and their willingness to participate. Rigidity stifles learning. Rules are a guideline--not a brick wall. We, as leaders, must determine whether the student is showing immaturity or rebellion with each infraction. Immaturity is to be trained. Rebellion is to be disciplined. If we discipline harshly against students who are immature and unclear on what we are expecting, we will create bitterness in their hearts. They will feel that it makes no difference whether they try or don't try to obey. To them, the response from the teacher is the same. If being good doesn't pay, then why make the effort?

Discipline in love will require each teacher to consider the individual as well as the rule. The same consequence can correct one student and crush another. Some teacher's feel that the student gets what he deserves. He asked for it, so he got it! However, correction followed by restoration must be our ultimate goal. To correct means to change behavior for the purpose of restoring right relationships within the classroom. The more we isolate and reject a student, the more we encourage him to isolate and reject us as teachers.

Circumstances outside the classroom may be at the root of today's misbehavior. Remain aware of mood changes due to family or social issues. Sometimes mercy is in order. A lighter punishment mixed with love and understanding may bring more correction at these times than the "normal" response.

Dear God, Give me the sensitivity to understand the individual needs of my students. Convict me when I am too stern or too lax. Teach me to love every student unconditionally and truly correct them rather than just punish them.

CR: Discipline, Restoration, Immaturity, Rebel, Mercy

67 I CAN'T AGREE WITH MY PRINCIPAL

Proverbs 11:2 *When pride comes, then comes disgrace, but with humility comes wisdom.*

Sometimes your principal may make a decision that you cannot accept or understand. You have two choices. You can accept the decision knowing that God is ultimately in charge, and ask God to direct your leaders. Or, if you feel strongly that the decision must be questioned for the good of the school, you can prepare an appeal and talk with your principal.

If you choose to appeal, consider the following thoughts to determine if you are properly prepared. If you have not been cooperative, have current unresolved conflicts or have recently shown resistance to your leader, you may not have earned the favor needed to ask for consideration. Have you consistently shown an attitude of respect and honor to your leader? If not, you probably should not try to make an appeal. Have you prepared a creative alternative to present to your leader when you ask that the decision be changed? Your principal will be more willing to hear your ideas when you offer a second solution. Is your solution in the best interest of the entire organization? If so, are you prepared to explain those benefits? Also, are you prepared to have your ideas rejected? You must give your leader the "right" to disagree with you. Avoid anger. It will destroy future favor.

Here's a word of advice--approach your employer with humility; respectfully present your concern and your creative solution. Show gratefulness for his/her willingness to hear your opinion. Don't be pushy or manipulative. End your meeting on a positive note thanking him/her for being willing to meet with you.

Dear God, Give me wisdom to know how to appeal to my employer. Help me to build a respectful attitude toward my principal even when I cannot understand or accept decisions. Build character in my life as I learn to submit to authority.

CR: Respect, Conflict, Authority, Boss, Appeal

68 OF WHOM SHALL I BE AFRAID?

Psalms 27:1 *The LORD is my light and my salvation--whom shall I fear? The LORD is the stronghold of my life--of whom shall I be afraid?*

I don't usually go out at night by myself. My husband, who normally went with me to our class forty-five minutes from my house, was unable to go this time. I prayed for protection and committed my trip to the Lord. The dark freeway was almost deserted. It was a new road and only a few cars were using it. About fifteen minutes into my trip, a car entered the freeway and advanced toward me at a high rate of speed. Since no other cars were around, I assumed the driver would pull to the other lane and pass me. Instead, he began to tailgate me and blink his lights. I continued to drive with the determination that I would not stop--no matter what. The car pulled beside me and began to honk the horn and flash the lights. I tried to locate a way of escape. The street lamps had not yet been installed; it was dark and deserted. There were no businesses at any of the exits. There was no escape. I could feel a terrifying fear surround me. I was afraid that I would lose the capacity to think. All of a sudden the words of a scripture song came to me. I began to sing them aloud. "The Lord is my light and my salvation, whom shall I fear?" As I sang, I felt my pulse slow down and peace surrounded me. I began to repeat—"Whom shall I fear? Whom shall I fear? God you will take care of me."

Of course, all of this happened in just a matter of moments. As I cried out for God to take care of the situation, the car pulled behind me again and exited the freeway without even slowing down. I continued on to school without incident, but my heart was filled with a special awareness of God's protection and constant care.

Scripture memory is a valuable assignment for our students. Whether it is memory quizzes or scripture songs, don't neglect to plant the Word of God in their hearts. Because of my knowledge of the above scripture, God was able to bring it to my memory to use as a weapon against the gripping fear and the lurking danger I was experiencing. Hebrews 4:12 states, *For the word of God is alive and active. Sharper than any double-edged sword...* It is the Sword of the Spirit of God--a weapon in the time of our need.

Dear God, Thank you for your supernatural protection. Forgive me for the times I have not respected and valued your WORD. Help me to be diligent in teaching them to my children, my grandchildren, and my students.

CR: Character Traits, Fear, Scripture Memory

69 THAT I MAY DWELL IN THE HOUSE OF THE LORD

Psalms 27:4 *One thing I ask of the LORD, this only do I seek: that I may dwell in the house of the LORD all the days of my life, to gaze on the beauty of the LORD and to seek him in his temple.*

David's devotion to God is reflected throughout the Psalms. He panted for God. His desire was to "dwell" with God every day in every situation. The appeal of the Psalms comes from the deep love and commitment the Psalmist had for his LORD.

Do you pant for God? Do you say to yourself, "I was glad when they said, 'Let us go to the house of the Lord!'"(Psalms 121:1) Or do you feel it is a strain to get up on Sunday and get to church? I'm meddling, now, but your relationship with God will affect your leadership with your students. You must be renewed spiritually to have spiritual life to pour out to others. An empty cup has nothing to spill out. A life filled with joy and the excitement of God will "win" others to Christ. Hebrews 10:22-25 says, *Let us draw near to God with a sincere heart and with the full assurance that faith brings, having our hearts sprinkled to cleanse us from a guilty conscience and having our bodies washed with pure water. [23] Let us hold unswervingly to the hope we profess, for he who promised is faithful. [24] And let us consider how we may spur one another on toward love and good deeds, [25] not giving up meeting together, as some are in the habit of doing, but encouraging one another—and all the more as you see the Day approaching.*

Draw near to God today. He's as close to you as your breath. Renew your commitment to prayer and Bible study. He calls you to His Secret Place with Him. Don't be embarrassed if it's been awhile. He's been waiting for you. Take your burdens, your frustrations, and your trials to His feet and leave them there. He cares for you and wants to set you free from the cares of the world. He invites you to come.

Dear God, Forgive me for neglecting the secret place. It's not that I don't want to pray and study the Bible. Life just gets so chaotic sometimes. Often I realize life gets hectic because I am not coming in prayer to leave my burdens. Today, I choose to come. CR: Prayer, Devotion to God

70 CHANGE MY LOUSY ROTTEN ATTITUDE (LRA)

Philippians 4:6-7 *Do not be anxious about anything, but in everything, by prayer and petition, with thanksgiving, present your requests to God. And the peace of God, which transcends all understanding, will guard your hearts and your minds in Christ Jesus.*

Ever had one of those days that your attitude was so rotten that you didn't want to talk to anyone for fear of blowing your Christian testimony? Perhaps today is one of those LRA (Lousy Rotten Attitude) days for you. There is a secret that I keep tucked away in my heart for those difficult times. I remind myself of words like--pray! Re-focus! God help me! *Create in me a pure heart, O God, and renew a steadfast spirit within me.* (Psalms 51:10). These have become reminders to me of where my help comes from. David proclaimed, *My help comes from the Lord!* (Psalms 129:8).

The first step is to recognize that I have the LRA. Second, I must search my heart for the root cause. Is it unforgiveness, anger, resentment, selfishness, pride, or unresolved conflict? Third, I must admit to God in prayer that I am holding on to the sin. Then, I need to release these harbored sins of anger to God and ask for grace and strength to forgive. Next, I ask for the peace of God to guard my heart and mind (Philippians 4:7). Lastly, I trust God and receive His peace.

Great formula! Don't you think? But sometimes, I just can't make it happen! What then? My answer always comes through the quiet times when I pull away from everything, put on music filled with proclamations of God's love, grace and awesomeness, and become still in His loving presence. This is the time I let God do his surgery on me. This is the time I need a new heart--a heart of love, a heart of flesh in exchange for a heart of stone and bitterness (Ezekiel 11:19). Only God can renew my spirit. Only God can heal me of LRA. It really doesn't take a long time--only a willing heart.

Dear God, Thank you for reminding me today that you are the answer to every problem I face--even my lousy rotten attitude. Give me a new heart. Change my struggle into peace and my anger into forgiveness and inner joy.

CR: Forgiveness, Thoughts, Heart Issues, Anger, Conflict, Attitude

71 I'M READY TO GROW UP

1 CORINTHIANS 13:11 *When I was a child I talked like a child. I thought like a child. I reasoned like a child. When I became a man, I put the ways of childhood behind me.*

Children, in their negative traits, are self-centered, stubborn, self-willed, rebellious (testing boundaries), unable or unwilling to reason with facts, easily angered, sneaky, gullible, destructive, undependable, fickle, rude, insensitive, and sometimes deceitful. On the other hand, their positive traits include being innocent, trusting, carefree, teachable, flexible, loyal, and forgiving. Scriptures give us two concepts regarding "putting away childish ways". The above verse clearly indicates that we are to move away from childish talking, thinking and reasoning. However, Jesus taught *that unless you change and become like little children, you will never enter the kingdom of heaven* (Matthew 18:3). Doesn't this seem to be a paradox?

While Paul encourages us to throw away the negative traits of childishness as we grow into complete maturity, Jesus reminds us to cultivate and grow even more in the positive traits of a child. The negative traits can be summed up in two words--self-centeredness and rebelliousness (the flesh). Paul encourages believers to crucify the flesh daily. We are to become willing to obey and follow God's commands and not our own desires. On the other hand, the positive traits are summarized in one word--trust. God is asking us to retain our child-like trust while we die to our selfish ways.

It is helpful to remind ourselves of the difference between children and adults. We cannot expect children to act as adults without training and maturity, but we MUST require mature action and thinking from ourselves. It makes sense that we, the adults, would have more tolerance and understanding of them than they would of us. We must be prepared to quietly and consistently train, reprove and correct as the situation requires. We must not condemn the child for being childish. We should accept him for where God has him--a child. We should continually require adult maturity from ourselves. God can help us when we are willing to ask Him for wisdom and understanding.

Dear God, I desire to be spiritually and emotionally mature. Remind me when I get angry or disheartened with my students. Help me to mature fully into the adult leader that pleases you.

CR: Maturity, Discipline, Leadership, Attitude

72 I WANT TO LEARN OBEDIENCE

1 Peter 2:13-14 *Submit yourselves for the Lord's sake to every human authority: whether to the emperor, as the supreme authority,* [14] *or to governors, who are sent by him to punish those who do wrong and to commend those who do right.*

Obedience is not always easy. In fact, many times it takes great fortitude to put aside your personal opinions and preferences to obey the things required of you by leaders. Have you ever felt that some rules were completely unrealistic or unnecessary? If you haven't, you are a rare specimen of the human race!

The key to obedience--willing obedience--obedience with a smile--inside as well as outside--is the phrase "for the Lord's sake". We must learn to obey those in authority over us graciously in preparation for the future assignments God has for us. If we cannot obey men's request, how can we obey God's difficult demands that may require even greater sacrifices?

See each trial as a proving ground to determine your willingness to obey. Luke 16:10 *Whoever can be trusted with very little can also be trusted with much, and whoever is dishonest with very little will also be dishonest with much.*

Another key is "Obedience with grace". We must each learn to be graciously obedient, serving our fellowman as unto the Lord. Our willingness to lay our life down for the brethren may be the key to someone's decision to follow graciously as well. Your students will be watching to see how you do when the principal makes a request of you. Will you be an example for them or will you prove to them that you teach one thing and live another. They are looking for genuine character. Somehow they will always know when you are not measuring up to your required assignments. God has his spotlight on you this year. You are on center stage. Perform "for the Lord's sake"; you will like the harvest that grows from the seeds that you plant!

One final thought, many have only obeyed when they are in agreement with the request. I believe the test of true obedience begins when you do what you are asked to do even though you do not want to do it, or you do not see the importance of the request. Many have never truly obeyed; they have only cooperated when they wanted to do what they were being asked to do. True obedience is a test of submission.

Dear God, Teach me the importance of submitting. I want to be a vessel of honor used for your service. Not my will but thy will be done. Teach me true obedience.
CR: Leadership, Authority, Obedience, Character Traits, Grace

73 TEACH ME TO CREATE THE BOND OF PEACE

Ephesians 4:2-3 *Be completely humble and gentle; be patient, bearing with one another in love. [3]Make every effort to keep the unity of the Spirit through the bond of peace.*

The atmosphere of your classroom will be determined by your attitude. A principal can feel the difference in classrooms when walking through the hallways. There are joyful, fun-loving teachers; strict, no-nonsense teachers; diligent detailed teachers; and quiet, gentle teachers. All of these personalities can be successful in the classrooms. But a teacher with a negative attitude, whether they are angry, unforgiving, uncaring, uninterested, or arrogant, will have difficulties in discipline.

Jesus told us that the greatest leaders among us would be great servants (Matthew 23:11). A teacher is a servant. We are called to serve, to teach, and to share the knowledge that God has so graciously allowed us to learn. Teachers must never have a proud spirit. Our age, education, and experience have equipped us. We must approach our classroom with humility, but also with confidence knowing that God has supplied us with a message to teach.

As conflicts arise, we must do our best to ponder our own childish mistakes from our past. This will help us find a balance in our discipline as we realize that many mistakes are due to immaturity, not rebellion. If a student is rebellious, we are to give firm discipline and encourage them to change the defiant behavior. If the student lacks understanding, or forgets, we must re-teach as we discipline. Two students can display exactly the same behavior for two different reasons--rebellion or immaturity. The only way we can determine which applies to the particular offense is to allow the student to explain.

Be patient and listen for what the student says "beneath" the explanation.

Love the child as you discipline. The Love of Christ can help you understand the student who challenges you repeatedly. He/she is a child. He/she is immature. He/she does not see events through the same seasoned, mature, experienced eyes that you do. Gently, lovingly, and firmly deal with students "for" their good" and, "for" their future. Draw from the love of God within you, and get rid of any negative emotions you have before you discipline. Teachers are the adults; students are the children. Pride can block your ability to do this. You must lay pride down and replace it with a grateful heart, full of humility and service to God's Kingdom.

Dear God, Discipline seems to be the hardest part of my job. I choose to lay down my pride and pick up a servant's attitude. Help me to learn your ways as I teach my students.

CR: Discipline, Rebel, Love, Attitude, Humility, Service

74 TEACH ME TO BE A PATIENT LEADER

Proverbs 14:29 *Whoever is patient has great understanding, but one who is quick-tempered displays folly.*

Unfortunately, many of us were not born with an easy-going temperament. Instead, we must build self-control through trials and tests. In the midst of these learning experiences we can count it all joy. Why? Because we can teach our students the secret of overcoming a temper as we conquer our own personal battles. The teacher who overcomes has a life message of victory. They can offer specific direction and counsel to students who struggle with similar temper difficulties. A patient teacher is loving, yet decisive, in control, understanding and wise. The godly character displayed in this teacher's life can help to equip students with skills needed to work with his/her fellowman.

"Sounds great, but I'm on the other end of the spectrum--the quick-tempered teacher. What do I do?" you ask. Perhaps you need to meditate on the "fruit" or result of a quick-temper. A quick-temper will:

1. negate your authority,
2. dull your Christian testimony,
3. be seen as a weakness by your class,
4. make your day to day experiences miserable for you.

Once students learn to push your buttons, they will play "the game" over and over again. The students secretly know that they win the battle when you lose your cool. They may even joke and make your temper a matter of conversation with other students. As a professional leader, you cannot afford the luxury of showing your anger.

Here are some suggestions that may help. Meet with your principal or a friend to discuss specific situations that stir up your anger. Seek counsel that may give you insights and solutions to the problem. Identify the student(s) who push your buttons and determine a plan of action for the next attack. For instance, you may decide that "Johnny—or Joni" will be placed out in the hallway anytime you feel anger building toward his/her behavior. It's better for the student to have "time out" than for you to lose your cool. You may discover that your discipline has not been methodical and consistent within your classroom. Correcting this may relieve the tension and regain the control needed.

Discipline is never you against the students. Rather it is the student against the rules or the students against your position (teacher). You are simply the policeman who writes out the ticket and gives the student what he has earned. Your emotions should not be involved. It is your responsibility to train your students. Teachers never "get back at a student." That is a child's approach. As an adult, you are to "train and reprove" and lead the student into more mature actions and thinking. Keep short accounts--don't let anger build. Pray for students who irritate you. Practice a controlled response privately when there is no conflict--rehearse for the real thing until the response feels more natural.

Dear God, Make me like you--patient, loving and firm. Give me the courage to discipline with purpose rather than anger. Teach me to act out of responsibility rather than react out of personal rights!

75 HELP ME TO FIND WISDOM IN ALL MY DOINGS

Proverbs 4:7-8 *Wisdom is the principal thing; therefore get wisdom: and with all thy getting get understanding.[8] Exalt her, and she shall promote thee: she shall bring thee to honour, when thou dost embrace her.(KJV)*

Those who walk in wisdom have learned to approach their daily lives through God's truths and His ways. It is imperative that we not only understand God's Word, but we must also understand its application to our specific conflicts each day. We must know the Word of God and hide it in our hearts. The depth and volume of the Word must be enough to serve as a resource when conflict comes. The deeper the knowledge, the greater the memorization, the more personal our experience is with God, the more likely we are to respond with the correct attitude and behavior pattern in times of stress. This takes a lifetime to develop. Perhaps that is why we hear so much about the older person having more wisdom; they have had more time and more experiences to develop their understanding and application.

A daily devotional time, just you and God, is a necessity for all of God's people, but it is especially important to those who are daily molding students' lives. You never know who will pattern their life after yours. You may even become their measuring sticks of what is right or wrong. Even though that may be a shocking and frightening reality, if we are honest, we will be able to look back to see adults in our lives, especially teachers, who either created a positive attitude or a negative, untrusting attitude toward the world in us. We must fill ourselves with God's truth daily. An empty vessel has nothing to pour out.

Dear God, Teach me the necessity of spending time with you. I must have your wisdom and your guidance in all of my day's activities. May I never forget the awesome responsibility that a teacher carries as innocent, simple children follow my leadership.

CR: Scripture Memory, Wisdom, Attitude, Conflict, Prayer, Leadership

76 I WILL TEACH MY STUDENTS TO OBEY

Ephesians 6.1-3 *Children, obey your parents in the Lord, for this is right.* [2]*"Honor your father and mother"--which is the first commandment with a promise--* [3]*"that it may go well with you and that you may enjoy long life on the earth.*

Current generations tend to no longer value obedience or consider it a necessary virtue. The "Me" generations have learned to evaluate "obedience" according to how it benefits their needs and desires. Many adults, as well as students, have never truly obeyed. Too many have only "agreed" with the request and obeyed because it seemed right to them. True obedience begins with doing what we are asked to do when it is not convenient, and we prefer not to do it.

Why should students obey? Ephesians 6:1-3 says because "it is right." And "that it may go well with [them]." Obedience is the foundation of character that all other positive traits are built upon. Children must learn to respect authority and must learn to obey without multiple warnings. Each time a student is allowed to disobey without consequences you have given permission to disobey. If students know that you know they disobeyed, you must take action. A reminder should be given only when you feel the student has really forgotten. If the behavior is repeated, consequences must follow.

Discipline is not for punishment, but, rather, it is to train the child to honor and obey authority. The best future leaders will have suffered the pain of obeying. Hebrews 5:8 states that although Jesus was the Son of God, he learned *"obedience by the things which he suffered"; (also Luke 2:51-52).* This suffering will build empathy and compassion for those who will follow their leadership in the future. Rebellious followers will grow into overbearing leaders.

There is a power play going on in your classroom. The children want to know who is going to win. Students push the rules until they know that the teacher wins. Secretly they know the teacher should win, but every teacher must establish his/her authority in the classroom by leading students to obey. Every child will not necessarily challenge the teacher's authority (thank goodness), but you will always have some students who will. The other students will be watching carefully to see who the winner will be. They care who wins.

As you teach students to obey, encourage cooperation from the parents as well. Teachers are coworkers with the parents. The school should never be an adversary. The teacher should always show respect to the parents (even if you have difficulties dealing with them). Support the home by communicating with the parents and soliciting their support. The child must know that the home and the school stand together. When this is not happening, ask your principal to join in a meeting with the parents. As a team, try to establish a plan on how to train the student. Most parents will cooperate if this is handled with respect, and if the teacher truly wants to work with the parents. When the student learns obedience, everyone wins including the student.

Dear God, Remind me that my students must obey. Correct me, as your child, when I begin to disobey you. Give me a servant's heart toward my students and their parents. And as I train their child, may I always remember I am a coworker with the parents. Teach me the importance of obedience.

CR: Discipline, Rebel, Communication, Parents, Coworkers, Obedience, Service

77 I NEED TO KNOW WHY I AM HERE

Ephesians 4:1-2 *As a prisoner for the Lord, then, I urge you to live a life worthy of the calling you have received.* [2] *Be completely humble and gentle; be patient, bearing with one another in love.*

There may be days when you question your choice of the teaching profession. Sometimes teachers feel that teaching is the most thankless, frustrating, self-sacrificing job there is on the face of the earth. We may even ask ourselves this question, "What did I do to deserve this?"

Jesus said, *I have chosen you...*" (John 15:16). You were created and designed by God to fulfill a purpose--God's 'calling' (Rom 11:29, 1 Corinthians 7:20). The calling God placed upon you is the very thing that makes you happy and fulfilled.

Search your heart; ask God to reveal to you His "calling" and then rest in that calling knowing that God will use the everyday routine to further His Kingdom. Lives are built lesson by lesson, bit by bit, day by day. Therefore, we often are unable to see growth in our students (and in us) for months and sometimes even years. We must yield ourselves to be vessels available for God's service. As we press toward God's will, the growth produced in our students and in us will be rewarding and satisfying.

Stand tall with determination and go forward with purpose--His calling! Get excited as you plan your lessons. God has already gone before you to prepare the way. In due season, you will reap (Galatians 6:9).

Dear God, Thank you for reminding me again that you have placed me in this job for this time in my life. Each of my students is part of my calling this year. Help me to keep my perspective free of muddle and self-pity. Again, I present myself as a living sacrifice for your service.

CR: Devotion to God, Rest, Serve, Sacrifice

78 HELP ME TO NOT BE NERVOUS DURING EVALUATIONS

Colossians 3:17 *And whatever you do, whether in word or deed, do it all in the name of the Lord Jesus, giving thanks to God the Father through him.*

Most teachers dread teacher evaluations, even experienced teachers. The thought of being graded and "written up" makes our knees knock and our heads reel. We fear criticism and rejection from our supervisor.

We must not allow ourselves to be overcome with fear. God is the greatest authority in our life. He is a constant companion throughout our daily tasks, and He knows the very desires of our heart. No success or failure goes unnoticed by Him. No gentle touch or harsh word goes unheard by the Creator of the Universe. As we do everything, word or deed, we should do it in the name of the Lord Jesus, Our ultimate goal is to please God.

If we please God, who is the highest authority, then anything a principal says will be secondary. We can welcome the comments and suggestions made by our principal when we understand that our supervisor is a tool from God sent to teach us a better way. You can have a calm, secure, and teachable spirit during evaluations because you want to be the best you can be. Like a child responds to a parent or a student to a teacher, you can respond to your principal with respect and a willingness to learn.

Get excited about your principal's visits to your classroom. You can look forward to learning new or better ways of doing things. Consider your principal working "for" you, not "against" you. Don't be rigid. If you are doing something out of the ordinary, like standing on top of your desk, when your principal walks into your class, continue teaching. You can give an explanation to your principal later. Don't feel guilty. Since your principal has been in the classroom, he/she will probably understand your explanation. If not, learn from the comments. If your supervisor chooses to suggest an alternate action for the future, accept his/her opinion and decide to follow the directives. You can become a better teacher as you submit to your principal's instructions and allow him/her to lead you. Any principal can teach you something! Of course, if you strongly disagree with your principal's requirements, you can always make an appeal. But, remember that appeals must always be done respectfully and privately. (See "Appeal" in the index.)

Dear God, Thank you for my principal and the instructions he/she offers to me. Help me to be pliable enough to learn from all instruction whether I immediately understand it or not. Teach me to welcome the principal's visits.

CR: Heart Issues, Leadership, Authority, Boss, Obedience, Attitude, Fear, Evaluations

79 HELP ME NOT TO BECOME WEARY IN WELL DOING

Galatians 6:9 *Let us not become weary in doing good, for at the proper time we will reap a harvest if we do not give up.*

Most jobs, sooner or later, become tiresome, less motivating, and/or difficult. There may be something about your job that makes you struggle, or there may be people on your team that steal the enjoyment of your job. Life is made up of struggle and reward. Pain and joy have been an interwoven expression of life for all time. In fact, without pain, joy seems mediocre; without struggle, reward is unappreciated.

As the days go by, the exciting beginning of school changes to the methodical schedule of day-in and day-out routine and progresses into the uphill climb of the century during the last quarter of the year. Remember "in due season" you will see benefit; don't faint!

During these difficult times, sleep more, eat right, exercise, and spend more time in prayer. Each of these will help to strengthen you for the climb. Try helping a fellow teacher who is struggling or overloaded. Turning your thoughts and energy outward to help another struggler can help you get your own struggles into perspective. As we give our time and energy to meet others' needs, God will restore energy and time to us. Try making a list of every project that needs to be done. Number those items according to what needs to be done (first, second, third, etc.) Next, begin to do each project in the order of priority. A sense of accomplishment will build as you begin to complete these smaller goals. Being overwhelmed and weary is often a signal of our need to re-focus our priorities, and change our current strategies. Consider postponing larger, long-term projects until spring or summer break when you have more time to concentrate and plan. If you see that you don't have the time or energy to try your new ideas this year, plan to start fresh with it next year.

Should you decide that you need to talk with someone concerning your struggles, choose a person with wisdom. Pity and agreement are not what you need. Pity may cause you to sink deeper into your pit. Seek wise counsel from someone who will be concerned, but also be realistic in helping you restructure your approach to your struggles.

Dear God. Teach me again to take my eyes off of my struggles and myself. Help me to refocus and set my eyes on the goal set before me. Give me wisdom through counsel for the issues I can't seem to overcome. My heart is to be a helping hand wherever I go--a servant of the Most High God. Lead me with your loving Spirit.

CR: Prayer, Devotion to God, Attitude, Serve, Thoughts

80 WHEN I AM WEAK, GOD IS STRONG

2 Corinthians 12:9-10 ... *"My grace is sufficient for you, for my power is made perfect in weakness." Therefore I will boast all the more gladly about my weaknesses, so that Christ's power may rest on me. [10] That is why, for Christ's sake, I delight in weaknesses, in insults, in hardships, in persecutions, in difficulties. For when I am weak, then I am strong.*

It has been said that God is more interested in my character than my comfort. I found this truth to be a solace as I struggle through each year's unique circumstances. Teachers often experience conflict, stress, disappointment, and fatigue during a school term. We must serve employers, our fellow teachers, parents, students, children, our families and churches. We work and live on a stage for all to critique. Our every move is closely regarded and our mistakes are often recorded. Our efficiency is evaluated and our children are tested. Under the close scrutiny of our audience, our weaknesses will become conspicuous. These are often the weaknesses we try hard to cover up, or the weaknesses we deny.

Scriptures tell us to humble ourselves, to accept the truth about our weaknesses, to submit under our leaders and ask for instruction and support, to lean on others, to ask God for wisdom, and to trust God for strength to overcome. We often respond with denial, excuse, anger, or pride when confronted with our failures. Remember that God's strength is made perfect in your weakness. Your lack may be a chance for someone to serve you as they use their unique gift. Or it could be an opportunity for you to see God's power manifested through your life. Your weakness can become your greatest strength as you allow "the power of Christ to rest upon you" and empower you with overcoming grace. God's grace is sufficient. His wisdom is awesome, and his Word is true. Let the nagging, despised, and hated reoccurring weakness in your life be a pivotal point of turning to God for strength. His strength is perfected in your weakness.

Dear God, I don't like to be weak, but if my weakness bends my knee toward your throne, I will be grateful. I know my perfection is in you alone. God help me in my struggle. Teach me to lean on you. CR: Grace, Attitude, Humility, Coworkers, Weakness

81 BUILD OUR STAFF INTO A TEAM FOR YOUR GLORY

Romans 12:3,10 ...*Do not think of yourself more highly than you ought, but rather think of yourself with sober judgment ...Be devoted to one another in brotherly love. Honor one another above yourselves.*

Basic principles of team building give us understanding of each member's responsibility.

Principle #1: Leaders are in charge because God placed them in that position. Even if the person climbed the success ladder using worldly tactics, it was God who placed them into leadership (Romans 13).

Principle #2: God sets teams together (Romans 4:16). Your coworkers were given to you by design.

Principle #3: God assigns workers to support and follow His leaders. They are to do work the leader asks them to do. (i.e. God gave Aaron and Joshua as helpers to Moses.)

Principle #4: Good followers are as important as good leaders. Both are needed to get the job done.

The leader's job is to train, equip and direct the staff. The staff's job is to learn and do the task. The leader may not be the most gifted among the staff. God places talented and gifted staff under a leader to fulfill the vision. Don't allow yourself to become jealous of others' gifts. God equips the team with variety to allow the whole to function properly.

When we see our leader out of step, we must pray for him. God can correct him; if he refuses, God may remove him. Leaders who misuse power will eventually lose their position. We must be careful not to use the world's weapons for correcting wrong. They bring shame to the body of Christ. In a Christian school, a church or any Christian organization, we must...

1. NOT sign petitions to build support for our grievances. God tells us to deal with offenses privately for the purpose of restoration and peace (Matthew 18:17). Mob rule is not God's way. Majority votes are not God's way. God promotes the

process of appeal. When you are given a directive and it is not against God's principles and your appeal is denied, obey your leader as unto the Lord.

2. NOT expose sin through the media. Scriptures tell us it is better to cover an offense. Use church discipline guidelines, and deal with sin as privately as possible. It may not be proper, at times, to involve all of the staff. (However, any illegal actions must be reported to police.)
3. NOT use the court system to settle disputes. Scriptures tell us to take our unsettled issues to Christian leaders who can help settle our grievances.

The Bible compares the church to a "body" with many parts and functions. Your teaching staff is also a "body". Each member should work together to protect and strengthen one another. When we battle within our staff, we overlook the real enemy. As we fight for our "rights" we are losing the war. United we stand; divided we fall.

Dear God, I want to follow your plan for my life and to always glorify your name. Give me the wisdom to work with this year's team .

CR: Coworkers, Respect, Obedience, Leadership, Rights, Unity

82 THE NAME OF THE LORD IS A STRONG TOWER

Proverbs 18:10 *The name of the LORD is a fortified tower; the righteous run to it and are safe.*

There is power in the name of Jesus. There is strength and renewal in the name of Jesus. There is deliverance and forgiveness in the name of Jesus. There is peace and contentment in the name of Jesus. His name is the name above all names.

A high school student once shared with me a horrifying experience she had while walking home from the store one afternoon. As she was walking, a man pulled up to the curb, jumped out of his car, and grabbed her arm. She instinctively cried out, "Jesus, help me. Save me." As she began to scream out the name of Jesus, the man became startled. He released her arm, ran back to his car, and drove away. This young lady entered into the Lord's strong tower. Some parent or teacher equipped her with trust in God.

One day a student fell in the gym and lost all feelings in both of his legs. Immediately the entire student body surrounded the young man and began to cry out to God for help without coaching or leading from the teachers. He was rushed to the hospital by ambulance and was released that afternoon without permanent injury. Someone equipped those students with the knowledge and wisdom to cry out to God in times of distress.

A phone call came into the office; my secretary answered it and began to cry. Her mom, who was visiting in Europe, had suddenly passed away. The teachers and students in the office quickly surrounded her and began to pray. One teacher continued the overseas conversation and gathered details about the incident as we comforted and prayed with our coworker. My secretary became calm and was able to finish the phone call. She had found the strong tower in Jesus, and ran into it for safety. What a blessing to have coworkers who can lead you into that refuge.

If allowed, teach your students to pray in the name of Jesus. Pray often with your children. Pray for their needs. In times of stress or disappointment or loss, pray with them. In times of victory, and rejoicing, pray with them. Let prayer be a normal part of your day--at home and (if possible) at school. Remember your students and children will model after you.

Dear God, You are a refuge, a hiding place. Teach us to run quickly into your arms for safety and renewal. Teach us to pray so that it becomes a natural response in times of need.

83 I CHOOSE NOT TO SIDE WITH THE TROUBLE MAKER

Romans 16: 17-18 *I urge you, brothers, to watch out for those who cause divisions and put obstacles in your way that are contrary to the teaching you have learned. Keep away from them. 18 For such people are not serving our Lord Christ, but their own appetites. By smooth talk and flattery they deceive the minds of naive people.*

There will always be those in your school who can find the negative in any situation and feel obligated to point it out. They often delight in stirring up strife and exposing error. In fact, they seem to get their significance by being the first to tell others about the problems. God's way is to overlook a wrong--to cover our brother's faults and help him overcome those faults. To delight in error shows a "fleshly" approach to life. Unfortunately, any of us can get caught in a critical attitude. We must consistently refuse bad attitudes and choose to overlook offenses.

Why should we avoid people who have critical spirits? We become like our friends. The scripture says that we should mark those who cause division. This means that we are to know their ways and never forget the destruction they bring to the Body of Christ. We are also reminded that even though they justify their words and give speeches dripping with honey coated words, their goal is to deceive the simple and to spread disharmony.

Mockers, critical persons, or rebellious followers must be recognized as a detriment to the school and confronted, avoided, or even removed from the school. Negative influences can come from students, parents, teachers, principals, board members, and, yes, even pastors. These stirrers may be completely unaware of their negative influence they are spreading. Gentle, loving confrontation may help the individual to see their error and save them from much unhappiness in the future. All of us have the capability of falling into this sinful pattern. Unforgiveness and bitterness are often the root causes of backbiting. These negative attitudes can be corrected when the problem is understood, and when the staff is willing to deal with it.

Dear God, Help me avoid a critical spirit. Do not let me become a mocker or a scorner to the authority you placed over me. Give me wisdom to recognize the evil about me and the courage to lovingly approach the problem when I see it in my school. CR: Division, Rebel, Mocker, Coworkers

84 LORD, I AM WILLING TO BE USED UP FOR YOU

Romans 12:1 ... *that ye present your bodies a living sacrifice, holy, acceptable, unto God, which is your reasonable service. (KJV)*

Teaching requires daily personal sacrifice. Teachers, much like parents, must measure their words and actions carefully in order to produce a positive influence in their students' lives. Irritability and a quick tongue can erase months of effective training. Unresolved conflict with parents, students, or coworkers can turn your school into a mini war zone. A master teacher does not put personal needs ahead of students' needs. Effective teachers must think before they act; they must purposely "act" rather than "react." This requires personal sacrifice.

Followers of Jesus should willingly go where they do not choose to go, to do things they prefer not to do, to put personal preferences upon the altar, and to die to their rights for the sake of Christ. Paul calls us to present ourselves as a sacrifice before God--a living sacrifice. God wants his servants to willingly crawl on the sacrificial altar and crucify ourselves (put to death our will) each day we live. Each morning we are to "present" ourselves before God as the daily "sacrifice"--a sacrifice of our will, our way, our desires, our preferences, our comfort and our plans.

A living sacrifice is a valuable tool in God's hands. Do you realize the full impact of someone completely surrendered as a "tool" for God's purposes? When we die to ourselves each morning, we are dead to our own will and free to seek God's will. We are released from our own expectations and agendas, and empowered to do the work of the Lord. Paul says that this is our "reasonable" service to God. Since Christ laid down His life for us, we are to also lay our lives down for Him.

Why do we cringe at the word "sacrifice"? We are flesh; we have physical desires and needs; we don't want to miss out on life; we have goals and desire success; we have preferences; we don't want to be strange--we want to be accepted; we don't like death--especially our own. Jesus said in Matthew 16:25 *Whosoever will save his life shall lose it; and whosoever will lose his life for my sake shall find it* (KJV). Death is the way to life!

Lord, I am willing to be used up for you. Give me the courage to crawl on the sacrificial altar today, to go the direction you choose for me and to follow you wherever you lead. Teach me how to die daily.

CR: Devotion to God, Service, Obedience, Sacrifice

85 GOD, TEACH ME TO BE AN EXAMPLE OF LOVE

John 13:34-35 *A new command I give you: Love one another. As I have loved you, so you must love one another. [35] By this everyone will know that you are my disciples, if you love one another.*

Jesus walked the dusty roads with impure disciples. They fussed; they competed; they disbelieved; they failed;

they denied him; and they even betrayed him. Jesus loved them in all their impurities; He saw beyond their imperfections; He saw their potential, what they could become, and He loved them. Jesus not only loved them in their unlovely, undeveloped stage, He trained them in character and spiritual maturity. He was not satisfied with just understanding the disciples' weaknesses. He sought to change those weaknesses into strengths. He was their teacher.

Today, if there is one student in your classroom that irritates you, that you can't think of anything good to say about, that you distrust, or that you have no hope for him/her, this scripture was written for you. Love wins; love brings change; love softens a hard heart; love is kind, considerate, and always hopes for change. Rejection builds barriers and walls; rejection brings destruction; rejection brings war; rejection kills hope; rejection insures failure. The scripture says, "...you MUST love one another."

You may be saying, "You don't know what they did." Or "They rejected me." A teacher is above his student. You have more life experiences, more maturity and more mistakes and victories from which to draw strength. Remember your own childhood mistakes. Give grace to your students--unmerited, undeserved acceptance. The longer you walk with God, the more you will see your "not so perfect attitudes and not so innocent motives". God wants to reveal to us our self-centeredness, our pride, and our stubbornness. Often when a student "pushes our button", an area of insecurity or pride within us is revealed. We can use these times of vulnerability to search our hearts, to repent, to learn, to grow and develop, and to mature in Christ. I have often wondered who learns the most through conflict--the teacher or the student. God uses conflict as a teaching tool to develop both student and teacher.

Students will remember who you are more than what you teach. They will recognize insincerity and double standards in a leader's life. As we teach them to love each other and to accept differences, we must guard ourselves to be sure that we are being consistent with our teaching. Unconditional love draws out the best in others. Love reflects our Savior. Love brings people to the foot of the cross. Love brings change.

Dear God. Forgive me for my lack of love toward students who are unlovely. Teach me to look beyond their faults and see their potential. Let love become a part of my daily walk with you.

CR: Love, Serve, Forgiveness, Leadership

86 HE SHALL DIRECT THY PATHS

Proverbs 3:5-6 *Trust in the Lord with all thine heart; and lean not unto thine own understanding. In all thy ways acknowledge him, and He shall direct thy paths.* (KJV)

The school year may not be going as you planned. Conflicts, and personal, financial or health issues may have unexpectedly stolen your joy. God has given us an answer for these times, "TRUST ME!"

Our plans are often destroyed by unexpected circumstances. We can maintain our inner peace and be determined to move forward again by reminding ourselves that God is in control. To trust God is to acknowledge Him in the twists and turns of our schedules. We make our plans, but God directs our paths (Proverbs 16:9).

Trusting is simple. To trust, you must let go! You must let go and let God have the right to lead you into any path He chooses. You must give up your right to have things perfectly laid out according to your plans. You must become the servant that follows his Master without complaint, without questions and without hesitation. To trust is to believe that God will always direct your paths correctly. It is to know that His plans are always for your good and not for evil, and to understand that no weapon formed against you can prosper (Isaiah 54:17)--long term.

How do you build trust in God? You can gain confidence in God by reading the Bible and understanding the work of God throughout history. As you reflect on your own life, you can begin to see the hand of God quietly, yet specifically directing your life. You will begin to relax and know that He is God. With this knowing--knowing that He is in charge--knowing that He sees the whole picture--knowing that He loves you unconditionally and wants good and not evil for you--knowing that He is not only your God, but also your Abba Father, you can begin to trust and lean on Him. He holds your future in His hands.

Are you weary and heavy laden today? Come to Jesus. Cast your disappointments, failures, hurts, and anger at His feet, for He cares for you. Leave your burdens and pick up His cross and follow Christ. His burden is light, but only when you allow Him to carry your future. Pray. Relax. Trust. Follow. Let God lead (Matthew 11:29-30).

Dear God, Thank you for your ability to see the whole picture---the beginning from the end. Teach me to trust you more. Today I cast my cares upon you. Forgive me for self-will and teach me to say "if God wills".

CR: Prayer, Trust, Devotion to God

87 SEND COWORKERS WHO LEAD ME TO A HIGHER PLANE

Proverbs 22:24-25 *Do not make friends with a hot-tempered person, do not associate with one easily angered or you may learn his ways and get yourself ensnared.*

Proverbs 29:8 *Mockers stir up a city, but wise men turn away anger.*

It only takes one disgruntled coworker to make the workplace a miserable daily grind, especially if that employee verbalizes his complaints in the teachers' lounge. Several years ago I was happy with my job assignment until they hired a woman with a critical attitude. After hearing her complaints against the leaders and the business day after day, I found myself liking my job less and less. Things that I never noticed before began to irritate me. Offenses began to grow. The job had not changed; my attitude had changed. I eventually found another job. Later I learned that the complainer stayed with that job for several years. She "talked" me out of my job!

I have seen this happen in schools. Teachers get angry and stir up other teachers and make everyone miserable. The grumbler may even stir up parents and students. Or, sometimes it's a student that becomes angry and stirs up other students. These things need to be corrected through loving confrontation. An unrestrained tongue (spark) can set a whole forest on fire (James 3:5).

Wise men turn away wrath; they do not socialize with angry men. You may be unable to stop others from complaining, but you can choose not to become part of the discussion. Simply excuse yourself from the conversation and leave the area. You may, in love, point out to the disgruntled worker how they are spreading bad seed and making themselves miserable. Coworkers can let the grumbler know that they don't want to hear the complaints. This confrontation may help the person deal with their attitude and unforgiveness. Your willingness to say something about their protests could make a difference in their year.

Take personal responsibility for the atmosphere of your school as far as it is in your power. Offenses are to be handled personally and privately. Purpose always to clear offenses, and never let a lot of time pass without settling your anger. Don't pick up the offense of a coworker. Instead, encourage them to go to the persons involved to resolve the conflict. These are God's instruction to the Body of Christ. As you follow them, you will be the winner!

Dear God, Let me choose to turn from anger. Help me to be part of the solution rather than part of the problem.

CR: Anger, Coworker, Tongue, Slander, Attitude

88 COMPARISON IS A BLACK HOLE

2 Corinthians 10:12 *We do not dare to classify or compare ourselves with some who commend themselves. When they measure themselves by themselves and compare themselves with themselves, they are not wise.*

Each teacher or staff member has unique gifts and callings. Together as a team, you are equipped to glorify God and accomplish His work for the year. Satan's tactic is to destroy your team through jealousy, competition, and/or comparison.

Comparison is a black hole-- a spiral leading downward toward bitterness and defeat. When I compare my strengths to someone's weaknesses, I become proud and arrogant. *Pride goes before destruction...* (Proverbs 16:18). When I compare my weaknesses to someone's strengths, I feel defeated and hopeless. If I compare my strengths to someone's strengths then I am in competition with them and unable to love them as myself. If I compare how much work I do with what they are doing, I often become offended and lose my zeal for the task. When I compare my righteous acts with the acts of others, I again become either proud or defeated.

God has called each of us to a particular task or ministry for *such a time as this* (Esther 4:14). We will live fulfilled lives if we serve God by "running the race" set before us--not "looking to the things behind us" or to the runners beside us--but by "pressing toward the mark" of pleasing God and excelling only for His pleasure and approval (Philippians 3:13-14). Only God knows his complete purpose and plan for today. Follow Christ and He will provide the affirmation you are seeking.

Dear God, Comparison is such a natural response to things that happen. Give me the wisdom to acknowledge my participation in this deadly cycle and the courage to turn from comparison and unhealthy competition with my fellowman. Restore the joy of serving to me as I release bitterness or defeat that has come from judgment and comparison.

CR: Comparison, Heart Issues, Coworkers

89 RESTORATION BUILDS GRATITUDE

Galatians 6:1 *Brothers and sisters, if someone is caught in a sin, you who are spiritual should restore that person gently. But watch yourselves, or you also may be tempted.*

A knock at the door interrupted my language lesson. I quickly assigned some work to my students while I spoke with the visitor. The parent and I stepped just outside the classroom and had a short conversation. Meanwhile, the noise level began to escalate in my classroom. I could tell things were getting out of control, so I excused myself and went back to my class.

I wasn't very pleased with my students. And, of course, I told them so. I lectured them about honoring visitors and being self-controlled and learning to be responsible. I gave them a warning about what would happen if this behavior ever happened again. Their eyes were wide and you could feel the tension in the room. I knew they had gotten my message. Now it was time to restore them.

As soon as I finished my lecture, I paused and just looked at them. I then took a deep breath and exhaled loudly and said, "Whew! Aren't we glad that's over with? Let's get back to work." Then I smiled.

The tension broke; you could see their muscles relax. Everything was back to normal. Puzzled, I watched silently as a girl stood up and came toward me. "We love you, Mrs. Wyrick," she said as she put her arms around me and hugged me. I smiled, patted her shoulder, and she returned to her seat.

I then understood the value of restoration. My students knew they were guilty. They were old enough to "know better". They were also immature enough to get caught up in a conversation and not think about it at the time. They needed forgiveness. My smile and release of tension through my words and body language communicated forgiveness to them. The young girl responded with gratefulness.

Restoration will be your spontaneous reaction when you turn your heart toward your students. Because I inwardly released my students from their immature behavior, restoration was a natural response. My students got my message; that was what I wanted. To do any more correction than that on a first offense would have been overbearing.

Dear God, Give me a forgiving heart toward others. Teach me to restore someone when it is obvious they know that they are wrong. Help me not to be a "nag"; instead let me lead them to the right path.

CR: Restoration, Forgiveness, Discipline

90 A SEASON AND A TIME FOR EVERYTHING

Ecclesiastes 3:2...a time to plant and a time to up root...

I remember my husband transplanting the small red bud tree in our front yard. It was such an exciting thing to watch the little sapling take root and begin to flourish. I enjoyed the cute purple blooms in the spring and the nice round leaves in the summer and fall. The tree developed perfectly in the spot next to the street. It became a landmark used to locate our house. My husband and I remarked several times about how pleased we were with our red bud tree. One day we noticed that the leaves on our tree were wilting. Full limbs were losing their leaves without cause. After inspecting the tree, my husband discovered that someone had used a drill with a one inch bit to bore a hole completely through the trunk of our red bud. Unfortunately, nothing could be done. Our tree withered and eventually was cut down and discarded. Where there once was a flourishing tree, now stands a few scraggly limbs that keep working their way up from the roots left in the ground to remind us what once had been.

As I age, it seems that experiences of decline and loss are becoming more plentiful. Recently, we lost dear friends in death, churches have closed, businesses have declined, and many around us struggle financially. My question to God becomes, "God how do I respond to so much decline and loss? Where are you in the midst of all the change I see in my life?"

God's quiet, gentle answer is simple. "I am in it all. I promised to never leave you, nor forsake you. Trust me, and keep following me. My way leads to life, not death." Turning to the Bibles, I was reminded of Elijah who sat by the water brook being fed by the Ravens. His comfort was not to last. One day his water brook dried up, and he was forced to leave. God was moving him forward. His circumstances required the move. God uses circumstances to move us forward toward our next purpose in life. We must not balk; we need to simply follow God's leading.

In your next crisis or disappointment, seek God's will in the situation. Give God time, and He can make all things beautiful for you. Remember, our joy is not in our circumstances, but it is in knowing Christ. Submitting to God's purposes and His will is the key to contentment and inner peace. God knows the times and the seasons of your life. Trust Him.

Dear God: I often find myself in the state of confusion or disappointment as I face difficult circumstances. Teach me to find your will in the midst of the changing of seasons and in the different times you have ordered for my life. I choose to trust you and follow you unconditionally.

SUBJECT INDEX